Recipes From Sandie's Galley

By Sandie Parker

A product of type**n**save™ software.

Copyright © 2007
Morris Press Cookbooks

All rights reserved. Reproduction in whole or in part without written permission is prohibited.

Printed in the U.S.A. by

P.O. Box 2110 • Kearney, NE 68848
800-445-6621 • www.morriscookbooks.com

Dedication

I would like to dedicate this cookbook to my friends and fellow boaters at Edward C. Grace Memorial Harbor, and to my special friend, LuAnn Meier, who was my inspiration.

Sandie Parker

Thank You

Special thanks to my husband, Jim, for all of his support, encouragement, and hard work in completing this book.

A sincere thank you goes to Kathy Salvatore, a new transient boating friend, for helping us with the cover design.

Last but not least, a very warm thank you to Tom Vranich, Editor of "The Elk Rapids News" in Elk Rapids, Michigan, and Robert Grnak, Editor of "The Township Times" in Saginaw, Michigan. They helped "Sandie's Galley" become a household name by running my recipes in their weekly newspapers.

Front Cover
Photo: Courtesy of Cruisers Yachts
2007 Model 497

About the Author

Sandie Parker lives aboard the "Nice N' Nauti" every summer. Her home port is the Edward C. Grace Memorial Harbor in Elk Rapids, Michigan. She works at the harbor designing and planting the flower gardens and landscape islands. Her newest project is an herb garden for the boaters.

Her husband, who tends to the business back home, spends long weekends on the boat, and often jokes: "what's wrong with this picture?"

Sandie was born and raised in Michigan. Her mother was always in the kitchen cooking and baking up a storm. She grew up with delicious family meals and desserts, every night of the week. She never knew then, that she would follow in her footsteps.

Working most of her life in the restaurant and country club business, her love for cooking took off when she met her mentor, Chef Carl Tanner. He taught her to think "outside of the box" and together they made a great team. His encouragement helped develop her confidence and her creative talent.

Sandie has won several cooking contests and has judged many others. Two of her favorite award winning recipes, "Louisiana Style Chili" and "Chocolate Lover Brownie Squares", are in this book. She is also the proud author of a recipe corner in two Michigan newspapers, titled (of course) "Sandie's Galley".

Cooking is now more than a career for her. It is a passion, as is her life with her husband, six adult children and two grand children. Many family memories were made throughout the years while sharing these meals together.

She hopes that these recipes will also bring you, your family and your friends wonderful meals and good times.....on a boat or anywhere!

Table of Contents

Breakfast 1

Appetizers & Munchies 5

Soups & Sandwiches 13

Salads & Vegetables 23

Poultry, Beef & Pork 35

Fish & Seafood 43

Sauces, Marinades
   & Dressings 47

Desserts 51

Specialty Drinks 59

Family Favorites 63

Index

Breakfast

Helpful Hints

- Over-ripe bananas can be peeled and frozen in a plastic container until it's time to bake bread or cake.

- When baking bread, a small dish of water in the oven will help keep the crust from getting too hard or brown.

- Use shortening, not margarine or oil, to grease pans, as margarine and oil absorb more readily into the dough or batter (especially bread).

- Use a metal ice tray divider to cut biscuits in a hurry. Press into the dough, and biscuits will separate at dividing lines when baked.

- To make self-rising flour, mix 4 cups flour, 2 teaspoons salt, and 2 tablespoons baking powder, and store in a tightly covered container.

- Hot water kills yeast. One way to tell the correct temperature is to pour the water over your forearm. If you cannot feel either hot or cold, the temperature is just right.

- When in doubt, always sift flour before measuring.

- When baking in a glass pan, reduce the oven temperature by 25°.

- When baking bread, you get a finer texture if you use milk. Water makes a coarser bread.

- If your biscuits are dry, it could be from too much handling, or the oven temperature may not have been hot enough.

- Nut breads are better if stored 24 hours before serving.

- To make bread crumbs, toast the heels of bread and chop in a blender or food processor.

- Cracked eggs should not be used because they may contain bacteria.

- The freshness of eggs can be tested by placing them in a large bowl of cold water; if they float, do not use them.

- For a quick, low-fat crunchy topping for muffins, sprinkle the tops with Grape-Nuts cereal before baking.

- Dust a bread pan or work surface with flour by filling an empty glass salt shaker with flour.

BREAKFAST

SCRAMBLED EGG BURRITO

8 eggs
1/4 c. milk
3 oz. Philadelphia cream cheese, softened
2 T. butter
1/3 c. onion, chopped
1/3 c. green pepper, chopped
1/3 c. chopped ham
1/3 c. Jacks salsa, drained
1/2 c. mozzarella shredded cheese
1/4 tsp. Montreal Steak Seasoning
4-6 flour tortillas
1 c. shredded cheddar cheese
Taco sauce

Beat eggs, milk and softened cream cheese with wire whisk until well blended; set aside. Melt butter in large skillet on low heat. Add egg mixture to skillet, cook until egg mixture begins to set, stirring occasionally. Add to egg mixture onions, peppers, ham, salsa, mozzarella, and steak seasoning. Continue to cook until eggs are fully set. To soften and warm the tortillas, place them in a 1 gallon size freezer bag with a few sprinkles of water on them. Leave bag open and microwave for 15 seconds. Spoon 1/2 cup of the egg mixture onto each tortilla, top with 1/4 cup shredded cheese and a tablespoon of taco sauce. Fold in opposite sides of tortilla, then roll up burrito-style. Serves 4 to 6.

POTATO PANCAKE

3 T. chopped fresh parsley
2 T. chopped onion
1 pkg. refrigerated shredded hash brown potatoes
1 egg slightly beaten with fork or whisk
3 T. flour
1/2 tsp. garlic salt
Pinch of pepper
4 T. olive oil
Sour cream

Chop parsley and onion, combine potatoes, and egg; mix. Combine flour, salt and pepper, sprinkle over potato mixture, and mix lightly. Heat 2 T. of oil in large fry pan over med. heat. Make potato patties the size of hamburgers, pat together well. Fry for about 9 minutes until dark golden brown, flip with spatula to brown other side until dark golden brown. Serve with a teaspoon of sour cream on the top. Serves 6.

EGG MUFFIN SANDWICH

1 English muffin
1 lg. egg for each
Salt & pepper to taste
1 slice Canadian bacon

1 slice American cheese
1 tsp. mayonnaise, mustard, or
   salad dressing

Place an English muffin ½ on a microwave plate, crack egg carefully on muffin, salt and pepper to taste. Microwave for 40 seconds on high. Place Canadian bacon and slice of cheese over egg. Spread mayo on other ½ of muffin and place on top. Microwave on high for 30 more seconds or until egg white is completely set and yolk has thickened around the edges.

OMELETTE FOR ONE

2 eggs, beaten
2 T. shredded Cheddar cheese
2 T. ham, diced
½ T. green pepper, chopped

½ T. onion, diced
Dash of McCormick's garlic
   pepper

Using a microwave safe mug, coat with a cooking spray. Combine all ingredients in a small bowl, pour into mug. Microwave on high for 1 minute. Stir, then cook an additional 1 to 1½ minutes more until eggs are set.

BACON SWISS QUICHE

1 c. Canadian bacon, diced
1 c. shredded Swiss cheese
½ c. sliced mushrooms, drained
1 T. dry minced onion

5 eggs
1 (5 oz.) can evaporated milk
¼ tsp. Montreal steak seasoning

Using a greased 9 in. micro-safe pie plate, layer Canadian bacon, cheese, mushrooms and onion. In a bowl beat eggs, milk and seasoning. Pour over layers. Microwave on high for 6 minutes, stirring twice. Continue cooking 2 - 3 more minutes until knife inserted in the center comes out clean. Let stand 5 minutes for the eggs to set. Serve in wedges.

EASY BREAKFAST BRUNCH

1 T. butter, melted
1 c. ham, cubed
½ c. green onion, chopped
¼ c. green pepper, diced

4 eggs, beaten
⅛ tsp. garlic salt
Pepper to taste

Pour melted butter into a 9 inch microwave safe pie plate. Add ham, onion and green pepper. Cover with wax paper and cook on high for 2 minutes. Stir in eggs, garlic salt and pepper. Cover and continue to cook on high for about 2 minutes or until a knife inserted in the middle comes out clean. Let stand for 3 to 4 minutes or until set. Cut into wedges. Serves 4.

Recipe Favorites

Recipe Favorites

Appetizers & Munchies

Helpful Hints

- You won't need sugar with your tea if you drink jasmine tea or any of the lighter-bodied varieties, like Formosa Oolong, which have their own natural sweetness. They are fine for sugarless iced tea, too.

- Calorie-free club soda adds sparkle to iced fruit juices, makes them go further and reduces calories per portion.

- For tea flavoring, dissolve old-fashioned lemon drops or hard mint candy in your tea. They melt quickly and keep the tea brisk!

- Most diets call for 8 ounces of milk and 4 ounces of fruit juice. Check your glassware. Having the exact size glass ensures the correct serving amount.

- Make your own spiced tea or cider. Place orange peels, whole cloves, and cinnamon sticks in a 6-inch square piece of cheesecloth. Gather the corners and tie with a string. Steep in hot cider or tea for 10 minutes or longer if you want a stronger flavor.

- Always chill juices or sodas before adding to beverage recipes.

- To cool your punch, float an ice ring made from the punch rather than using ice cubes. Not only is this more decorative, but it also inhibits melting and diluting.

- Place fresh or dried mint in the bottom of a cup of hot chocolate for a cool and refreshing taste.

- One lemon yields about ¼ cup juice; one orange yields about ⅙ cup juice. This is helpful in making fresh orange juice or lemonade!

- Never boil coffee; it brings out the acid and causes a bitter taste. Store ground coffee in the refrigerator or freezer to keep it fresh.

- Always use COLD water for electric drip coffee makers. Use 1 to 2 tablespoons ground coffee for each cup of water.

- Seeds and nuts, both shelled and unshelled, keep best and longest when stored in the freezer. Unshelled nuts crack more easily when frozen. Nuts and seeds can be used directly from the freezer.

- Cheeses should be served at room temperature, approximately 70°.

- To prevent cheese from sticking to a grater, spray the grater with cooking spray before beginning.

APPETIZERS & MUNCHIES

BACON WRAPPED SHRIMP OR SCALLOPS

2 T. lemon juice
½ tsp. Creole seasoning
¼ tsp. garlic salt, Lawry's is the best
18 uncooked, fresh or frozen but thawed jumbo shrimp, shelled & de-veined; or

18 fresh or frozen but thawed Scallops, rinsed or 9 of each
9 slices bacon, halved

Mix lemon juice, Creole, and garlic salt, stir in seafood, cover and seal. Meanwhile cook bacon lightly in microwave or fry pan, turning once. Drain on paper towels. Wrap a ½ piece of bacon around each shrimp or scallop, toothpick together. Discard marinade. Grill on med. heat 4 to 7 min. or until shrimp is pink and scallops are opaque and bacon is crispy brown. Alternative: omit the marinade and base BBQ sauce on them, cook the same way. See "Sauces". May also use water chestnuts, if you desire. Serves 4.

YUMMY PIZZA DIP

1 (8-oz.) container of chive and onion cream cheese spread
½ tsp. oregano
¼ tsp. garlic salt
½ c. pizza sauce

½ c. chopped green pepper
½ c. chopped ham or pepperoni
½ c. shredded mozzarella cheese
½ c. shredded cheddar cheese
Bagel chips or crackers

Layer cream cheese spread in a microwave safe 9 in. pan, sprinkle with oregano and salt. Layer the rest of ingredients in order. Microwave on high or until cheese has melted. Oven alternative: Bake in ungreased 9 in. pan at 350 degrees, for 10 to 15 minutes Serves 6.

BLT DIP

- 1 (8-oz.) pkg. Softened cream cheese
- 1/2 c. ranch dressing
- 1 med. tomato, seeded and chopped
- 6 slices cooked bacon, crumbled, or 2 oz. of cooked real bacon pieces (Hormel)
- 1/2 c. finely chopped celery
- 2 T. finely chopped onion
- 1 tsp. sugar
- Lettuce leaves
- French Bread toasted, crackers or bagel chips

Cream together cheese and ranch dressing. Add the rest of the ingredients except the lettuce and the toast. Mix together. Spread lettuce leaves in a small serving bowl, fill with dip, and garnish with a few pieces of chopped tomato. Serves 4-6.

CRAB FONDUE

- 16 oz. soft cream cheese
- 2/3 c. mayonnaise
- 1/8 c. white wine
- 3 (2.5 oz.) pkgs. premium crab meat, drained
- 2 tsp. chopped chives
- 1/2 tsp. prepared mustard
- Pinch of seasoning salt
- Dash of garlic powder
- 1/4 tsp. Worcestershire sauce
- French bread or crackers

Melt cream cheese and mayo in a microwave-safe bowl. Cook 1 to 2 minutes on high, stirring once. Add wine, stir again, then add the rest of the ingredients and mix together. Place in a fondue dish or a small crockpot on low. Serve with bite size pieces of French bread using fondue forks or use a spoon with crackers.

BEEF ROLL-UPS

8 oz. softened cream cheese
3 tsp. creamy horseradish sauce
6 thin slices plum tomatoes
40 sm. thin slices seedless cucumber
1 thin slice purple onion
8 (6-7 in.) wheat tortillas, or flavor of your choice
½ lb. thinly sliced deli roast beef

Combine cream cheese and horsy sauce, mix well. Spread evenly on each tortilla, about 2 T. on each. Top with layer of sliced tomato, cucumber slices, 3 onion slices and 1 to 2 roast beef slices. Roll tortilla tightly, repeat with each tortilla. Wrap them in plastic and refrigerate, seam side down for at least 30 minutes. Cut each in 3's crosswise and serve. Makes 24.

VEGGIE SNACK SAUCE

1 c. olive oil
¼ c. wine vinegar
½ c. sugar
1 tsp. celery seed
1 tsp. salt
1 T. onion powder
1 tsp. paprika
1½ c. broccoli flowerets
1½ c. cauliflower, bite size pieces
1½ c. mushrooms
1½ c. mini carrots

Mix everything except veggies and let stand 1 hour, then stir. Place veggies in a large bowl. Pour sauce over veggies when ready. Mix thoroughly, store in refrigerator for 2 hours, drain and serve. Yummy and oh so healthy! Serves 4- 6.

JUMBO SHRIMP WITH HOME MADE COCKTAIL SAUCE

1 bottle chili sauce or 1 c. Ketchup
1½ T. horseradish, or to taste
1½ lbs. frozen thawed or fresh cooked shrimp, tail on but shelled

Mix the chili sauce and horseradish together, put in small bowl, and serve with chilled shrimp. Serves 6.

GUACAMOLE & CREAM CHEESE DIP

1 (8-oz.) tub of soft cream cheese
8 oz. guacamole
8 oz. bruschetta
8 oz. shredded cheddar cheese

Layer in order, ending with cheese in an 8 x 6 x 2 inch glass dish. Serve with Frito Scoopers, or Tortilla chips. Easy and good! Serves 4.

PROSCIUTTO AND MELON CANAPAS

2 tsp. minced garlic
1/2 lb. soft butter
3 drops Tabasco sauce
4 drops lemon juice
Melba toast or baguettes, toasted
6 oz. thinly sliced prosciutto
1/2 cantaloupe cut into 1 in. wide pieces
Fresh basil or dill snips

Mix together garlic, butter, Tabasco sauce and lemon juice. Spread garlic butter over toast, top with a slice of prosciutto and a piece of cantaloupe, sprinkle with a few drops of lemon juice. Season with a pinch of basil, or dill. Serves 4.

SALMON DILL MINI SANDWICHES

1/4 c. sour cream
1/3 c. ranch dressing
6 oz. cream cheese, softened
2 tsp. fresh dill weed, chopped
2 tsp. lemon juice
20 cocktail pumpernickel bread slices
1 med. seedless cucumber, cut 40 thin slices
1/2 lb. smoked salmon, cut in 1 in. cubes
Lemon peel

Mix sour cream, ranch dressing, cream cheese, dill and lemon juice in a small bowl. Spread mixture evenly onto bread slices. Top with 2 slices of cucumber and a small piece of salmon. Sprinkle a touch of lemon peel on top. Makes 20 mini sandwiches.

DILLY DIP FOR VEGETABLES

1 c. Hellmann's mayonnaise
1 c. sour cream
1 T. parsley
1 T. Dill
2 T. chopped onion
1 T. accent
1 tsp. sugar

Mix together and refrigerate for at least 3 hours before serving. Serve with raw vegetables!

CREAMY DILLED SHRIMP

1 1/2 c. Hellmann's mayonnaise (Canola)
1/8 c. sugar
1/2 c. sour cream
1/2 c. red onion, sliced
1 T. fresh dill
1 1/2 lbs. frozen jumbo shrimp, thawed and remove tails

In lg. bowl mix all ingredients. Cover and refrigerate overnight. Serve with toothpicks. Serves 4 - 6.

BOATERS CUCUMBER DILL DIP

1 (8 oz.) pkg. softened cream cheese
1 c. lite mayonnaise
1 seedless cucumber, peeled and chopped small
2 T. green onion, diced
1 T. lemon juice
2 tsp. fresh snipped dill weed
1/2 tsp. hot pepper sauce

Beat cream cheese until smooth. Stir in remaining ingredients until well mixed. Cover and chill. Serve with fresh veggies, or bread sticks. Makes 2 1/2 cups.

MICROWAVE PEANUT BRITTLE (SO EASY!!!)

1 c. sugar
½ c. light corn syrup
1 c. salted peanuts
1 tsp. butter
1 tsp. vanilla
1 tsp. baking soda

Butter cookie sheet, set aside. Mix in microwavable bowl the sugar and corn syrup, microwave for 4 minutes. Add peanuts, then microwave for another 3½ minutes. Now stir in butter and vanilla, microwave another 1½ minutes. Stir in the baking soda, and then pour on the cookie sheet. Let cool, then break into pieces.

OYSTER CRACKER SNACK

1 sm. envelope dry Italian or
  Ranch salad dressing mix
1 T. dill weed
½ c. canola oil
1 T. garlic powder
2 pkgs. Premium oyster crackers

Mix the pkg. of dressing, dill, oil and garlic powder in the measuring cup until blended well. Using a paper grocery bag, pour crackers inside and drizzle the oil mixture on top. Close the bag tightly, hold with hands and shake gently, until all the crackers are coated well. Pour the finished product into a gallon size freezer bags, or a sealed plastic container.

CHOCOLATE NUT CLUSTERS

2 c. semi sweet chocolate chips
¾ c. white chocolate chips
¾ c. milk chocolate chips
2 T. butter
1½ - 2 lbs. mixed nuts, or
  peanuts.

Using a medium bowl, microwave the chocolate and the butter on full power for 1- 2 minutes, or until melted. Stir well until smooth. Add nuts, stir together until coated. Drop by teaspoon onto wax paper. Let stand until cooled and hardened. May store for 3 weeks in a closed container if kept cool. Separate layers with waxed paper.

NUTS AND BOLTS

1 box Crispix cereal
1 box Corn Chex
1 box bran or Wheat Chex
1 box Cheez-its
1 bag bite size pretzels

2 lbs. mixed nuts
1¼ lb. butter, melted
1 heaping T. garlic salt
2 heaping T. garlic powder
4½ tsp. Worcestershire sauce

Using the top and bottom of a large rectangular roaster, split the cereal and crackers in half and mix gently. Melt the last 4 ingredients together and spoon evenly onto the cereal mixture. Stir carefully. Bake in a 250° oven for 2 hours, stirring every 15 minutes. Allow to cool and package in closed containers.

GRANOLA FRUIT SNACK

4 c. Granola cereal with almonds
1 c. salted peanuts, or almonds
1 c. dried banana chips
1 c. dried cherries, or cranberries

3 T. butter
3 T. honey
½ tsp. cinnamon
¾ c. flaked coconut

Heat oven to 325°. Mix granola, nuts, banana chips and dried cherries in a lg. bowl. Heat butter and honey over low heat until melted. Add cinnamon, stir. Pour over cereal mixture and mix. Spread into a 15 x 10 baking pan. Bake 15 minutes, stirring once. Remove from oven, stir in coconut, then let cool for 15 minutes. Loosen from pan and store in gallon size freezer bag. Makes about 8 cups.

CHOCOLATE MALT SNACK MIX

2 c. Corn Chex cereal
2 c. Rice Chex cereal
2 c. Crispix cereal
1 c. cocktail peanuts
1 c. semi-sweet chocolate chips
¼ c. butter or margarine
¾ c. malted milk powder
1½ c. coarsely chopped malted milk balls

In large bowl, mix cereals and peanuts. In 1-quart saucepan, heat chocolate chips and butter over low heat, stirring occasionally, until melted and blended. Pour over cereal mixture, stirring until evenly coated. Gradually stir in malted milk powder until evenly coated. Stir in malted milk balls. Cool by laying out on waxed paper. Store in airtight container or freezer bag.

PUPPY CHOW

1 (12 oz.) bag semi-sweet chocolate chips
½ c. butter
½ c. peanut butter
9 c. Chex cereal, rice or corn
2 c. powdered sugar

Combine chocolate chips, butter and peanut butter together in a bowl and microwave on high for 1 minute. Stir, return to microwave for 10 to 20 seconds until melted thoroughly. Pour mixture over Chex cereal and mix gently until coated. Put powdered sugar in large paper bag and add cereal mix. Shake until coated. Place on waxed paper to dry.

Recipe Favorites

Soups & Sandwiches

Helpful Hints

- Fresh lemon juice will remove onion scent from hands.

- To save money, pour all leftover vegetables and water in which they are cooked into a freezer container. When full, add tomato juice and seasoning to create a "free" soup.

- Instant potatoes are a good stew thickener.

- Three large stalks of celery, chopped and added to about two cups of beans (navy, brown, pinto, etc.), will make them easier to digest.

- When cooking vegetables that grow above ground, the rule of thumb is to boil them without a cover.

- A lump of sugar added to water when cooking greens helps vegetables retain their fresh color.

- Never soak vegetables after slicing; they will lose much of their nutritional value.

- Fresh vegetables require little seasoning or cooking. If the vegetable is old, dress it up with sauces or seasoning.

- To cut down on odors when cooking cabbage, cauliflower, etc..., add a little vinegar to the cooking water.

- To avoid tears when cutting onions, try cutting them under cold running water or briefly placing them in the freezer before cutting.

- Perk up soggy lettuce by soaking it in a mixture of lemon juice and cold water.

- Vinegar can remove spots caused by tomatoes. Soak the spot with vinegar and wash as usual.

- Egg shells can be easily removed from hard-boiled eggs if they are quickly rinsed in cold water after they are boiled. Also, add a drop of food coloring to help tell the cooked eggs apart from the raw ones in your refrigerator.

- Keep bean sprouts and jicama fresh and crisp up to five days by submerging them in a container of water, then refrigerating them.

- Your fruit salads will look perfect when you use an egg slicer to make perfect slices of strawberries, kiwis, or bananas.

SOUPS & SANDWICHES

SANDIE'S BAKED POTATO SOUP

12 med. potatoes, bake, or microwave, peel and mash
3½ c. milk
½ c. butter or margarine
(8-oz.) sour cream
1½ c. water
½ lb. cooked bacon pieces or 1 bag Hormel real bacon
3 green onions, chopped
1½ tsp. garlic salt
2 c. shredded cheddar cheese
½ tsp. celery salt
1 T. sugar
1 T. parsley flakes
2 tsp. worcestershire sauce
½ c. Hidden Valley ranch dressing

Mix well and heat on low for 40 minutes, stirring frequently. If it gets too thick, you may add a little more water or milk. Serve with a fresh parsley garnish. Makes 6- 8 bowls.

CREAM OF BROCCOLI SOUP

1 pkg. frozen broccoli
1 c. water
2 T. butter
2 c. Velveeta cheese, cubed
2 c. milk
1 c. half & half
¼-½ c. wondra
1 c. chicken stock

Using a large saucepan, cook broccoli in the water until good and hot. Do not drain. In a separate sauce pan, combine butter and cheese. When melted add to the broccoli, stir well. Add the rest of the ingredients, stirring over medium heat until hot and thick. Serves 4-6.

FRENCH ONION SOUP

½ c. butter
6 lg. sweet onions, chopped in large pieces
½ tsp. garlic salt
6 (10¾-oz.) cans beef consommé
3 (10¾-oz.) cans water
1 c. dry white wine

1 T. worcestershire sauce
Parmesan cheese, grated
Mozzarella cheese, shredded
Lg. seasoned croutons, or round toast
Swiss cheese slices

    Melt butter in large fry pan, add chopped onions and garlic salt, cook until onions are tender. In a lg. pot pour in consommé, water, wine and worcestershire sauce, stir. Add cooked onions and butter, simmer for 2 hours. For serving, pour soup into a crock, sprinkle 1 T. Parmesan cheese and 2 T. Mozzarella, then add piece of toast, or a handful of croutons, top with a slice of Swiss cheese, broil near top of oven until Swiss cheese is golden brown. You may also microwave in crock, if you do not need the cheese to be browned.

CREAM OF TOMATO SOUP

1 (14-oz.) c. chicken broth
1 T. finely chopped onion
½ tsp. minced garlic
⅛ tsp. ground black pepper
1 tsp. celery flakes
1 (14-oz.) c. stewed tomatoes, blended

1 (10¾-oz.) c. condensed tomato soup
1 T. sugar
1 c. whipping cream
4 oz. soft cream cheese
2 T. butter

    In a large saucepan combine first 5 ingredients. Bring to boil, simmer for 6 min. Add blended stewed tomatoes and soup. Bring to boil. Simmer, uncovered for 20 min. Stir in whipping cream, softened cream cheese and butter. Heat through. Makes 4-6 bowls.

YUMMY CHEESE AND BLACK BEAN SOUP

1 (16-oz.) pkg. Velveeta cheese, cut into cubes
1½ c. milk
1 (11-oz.) can corn, drained
1 (15-oz.) can black beans, rinsed and drained
1 (14-oz.) can diced tomatoes with green chilies, undrained
¼ c. chopped onion
¼ tsp. garlic salt
⅛ tsp. Montreal Steak Seasoning
Chopped fresh cilantro

In a large saucepan, melt cheese with milk over med-low heat, stirring while cheese is melting. When it is creamy stir in the rest of the ingredients except cilantro. Simmer 30 minutes. Serve with sprinkles of cilantro on top. Makes 6-8 bowls.

VEGETABLE BEEF & BARLEY SOUP

1 lb. round steak
1 med. onion, chopped
2 T. butter
2 (14-oz.) cans beef broth
2 (14-oz.) cans Italian style diced tomatoes
3 c. water
½ c. chili sauce
¼ tsp. garlic salt
4 c. coarsely chopped cabbage
1 c. celery, bite size pieces
1 can corn, drained
1 c. quick barley

Cook together steak, onions and butter. Place in soup pot and add broth, tomatoes, water, chili sauce and garlic salt. Bring to boil, then add the rest of the ingredients. Simmer for 20 minutes or more. Serves 6-8.

SIMPLE MINESTRONE SOUP

2 lg. cans Chunky brand chili
1 (14-oz.) can diced tomatoes
1 (10¾-oz.) can beef consommé
1 (10¾-oz.) can water
1 pkg. frozen corn
1½ c. celery, cut in bite size pieces
1 T. worcestershire sauce
1 tsp. minced garlic
¼ c. sugar
1 tsp. dried basil
½ tsp. cilantro
½ tsp. garlic salt
½ tsp. Montreal steak seasoning
½ c. small pasta
1 (14-oz.) can kidney beans

You are going to love this part, place all ingredients into a soup pot, mix well and simmer for 1 to 2 hours. Serves 6.

SANDIE'S AWARD WINNING LOUISIANA STYLE CHILI

1 med. onion chopped
6 celery stalks, sliced
2 T. butter
5 c. cooked, diced chicken (breasts are best)
1 lb. cooked bacon, cut into pieces
1 head cabbage, cored and chopped
2 c. sliced mushrooms
3 cans dark red kidney beans, drained

Broth:
1 gal. chicken broth
½ c. chicken soup base, mixed with ½ c. hot water
1 (18 oz.) bottle Baby Ray's BBQ sauce
1 (24 oz.) bottle Ketchup
¼ c. liquid smoke, hickory flavor
⅔ c. sugar
1 ½ T. garlic salt
2 T. Worcestershire sauce
1 T. Montreal steak seasoning
Tabasco sauce to taste

Sauté onions and celery in butter. Place in 5 qt. soup pot. Add all of the broth ingredients stir and then add the rest. Mix well. Cook over low heat for 4 hours or more stirring occasionally, or in a crock-pot all day on low. Serves 8-10.

CHICKEN NOODLE SOUP

5 chicken breasts
1 med. onion, chopped
5-6 stalks of celery, chopped
½ stick butter
1 pkg. wide noodles, cooked
2 c. broth from cooking the chicken

2 (32 oz.) boxes of chicken broth
4 T. chicken base, or to taste
1 T. garlic salt
2 T. fresh cut basil, or 1 tsp. dried basil

Cook chicken breasts in enough water to cover them until done, save 2 cups of broth. When cool enough to touch, cut chicken up into bite size pieces. Sauté onions and celery in butter. Cook noodles a few minutes less than directed. They will continue cooking in the soup. Drain when done. Place all ingredients in large soup pot, stir gently, cook on med heat until hot, then simmer for 1 hour. You may add carrots also. Serves 8-10.

MY SPECIAL ITALIAN SAUSAGE SOUP

1 lb. ground chuck, brown and drain
1 lb. ground Italian sausage, brown and drain
1 head cabbage, chopped
6 stalks chopped celery
3 (14 oz.) cans diced tomatoes with chilies
1 (32 oz.) box of beef broth
1 (14 oz.) can beef consomme
1 (14 oz.) can of water
1 T. garlic juice
1 T. minced garlic
1 tsp. paprika
1 tsp. The Chefs Miracle Blend, or McCormick's Montreal Steak Seasoning
1 tsp. garlic salt
4 T. sugar
1 can mushrooms, drained / optional

Here comes the easy part, place everything together in a crock pot or large soup pot. Stir well simmer for 1 to 2 hours on low, or if in crock pot cook on low for 6 hours or more. Serves 6-8.

CHICKEN GUMBO SOUP

1 med. onion, chopped
2 T. butter
3 lbs. cooked chicken, cubed
1 (32-oz.) box chicken broth
2 (10¾-oz.) cans chicken broth
1 T. chicken base
2 carrots, pared and sliced
½ c. celery, sliced
1 bay leaf
2 tsp. parsley
1 c. frozen corn
1 c. frozen peas
1 c. frozen okra
½ lb. fresh, mushrooms, quartered
2 (14-oz.) cans Italian stewed tomatoes
½ tsp. basil
1 T. sugar
Salt & pepper to taste

Sauté onions in the butter in a small skillet. Place this into a large pot and add the rest of the ingredients, stirring as you add them. Cook for 1 hour on low, or in crock pot all day long on low. Makes 6-8 servings.

SANDIE'S UNIQUE TACO SOUP

2 lbs. ground round
1 onion, chopped
2 (14 oz.) cans diced tomatoes with chills
1 (30.5 oz.) can Brooks mild or hot chili beans
1 (1 lb.) bag corn, frozen
2 (14-oz.) cans beef broth
2 (1.25 oz.) pkgs. taco seasoning mix
2 (1.25 oz.) pkgs. ranch dressing mix
½ c. Hidden Valley Ranch Dressing
1½ c. shredded cheddar cheese, divided
1 c. shredded lettuce, divided
Dollops of sour cream
Taco sauce, to taste
Corn chips

In large skillet brown beef and onions, drain. Place in soup or crockpot. Blend tomatoes in blender, add to the beef. Then add beans, corn, broth, seasoning packets and ranch dressing. Stir well and cook on low for 30 minutes or more. Top with shredded cheese, lettuce, a dab of sour cream, a drizzle of taco sauce, and chips. Serves 6-8.

SMOKED SEAFOOD GUMBO

¾ c. chopped onion
1 lb. smoked sausage, cut in bite size pieces
1 T. olive oil
¼ c. wondra or cornstarch
6 c. cooked chicken breasts, cubed
1 can crabmeat, drained
2 (14-oz.) cans diced or stewed tomatoes
1 c. chicken broth
1 c. celery, sliced
2 tsp. oregano
2 tsp. thyme
½ tsp. pepper flakes
¼ c. sugar
1 tsp. garlic salt
1 tsp. Creole seasoning
⅓ c. orzo, plain or trio
1 pkg. thawed frozen shrimp, shelled and no tails

In small skillet cook onions and sausage in oil, add wondra, cook 3 to 4 minutes until wondra or cornstarch begins to brown. Reduce heat, stir until smooth. Combine all other ingredients except shrimp in a large pot, add sausage mixture to this. Stir well until mixed. Cook on low for 1 hour. Add shrimp 10 minutes before serving. Serves 8.

CHICKEN OR TURKEY ALFREDO SOUP

1 c. broccoli, chopped
½ c. carrots, chopped
½ c. onions, chopped
1 c. frozen corn
1 c. sliced canned mushrooms, drained
1 tsp. minced garlic

28 oz. chicken broth
½ tsp. garlic salt
¼ tsp. steak seasoning
½ tsp. dried basil
2½ c. diced cooked chicken or turkey
1 (16 oz.) jar Alfredo sauce

Using a 5 qt. sauce pan combine everything except poultry and Alfredo sauce, mix well. Bring to boil, simmer, add chicken or turkey and Alfredo sauce. Stir well and heat thoroughly. Serves 6.

MY EASY HAM AND BEAN SOUP

1 sm. onion, chopped
6 stalks celery, sliced
¼ c. butter
1½ lbs. diced cooked ham
2 tsp. minced garlic
1 tsp. garlic juice
32 oz. beef broth
2 (10½ oz.) cans beef consumme
3 (15.5 oz.) cans northern beans

2 (14.5 oz.) cans diced tomatoes with chilies
3 T. fresh chives
¾ c. Sweet Baby Ray's BBQ sauce, hot and spicy
2 T. sugar
½ tsp. dried basil
1 (15 oz.) can sweet corn with peppers

Using a 3 qt. sauce pan sauté onions and celery in the butter. Add the rest of the ingredients, stir well. Cook over med. heat for 30 minutes, then simmer for an hour, occasionally stirring. Serves 8 or more.

ORIENTAL SHRIMP SOUP

2 (14-oz.) cans chicken broth
2 c. zucchini, cut in sticks
2 green onion, sliced
1¼ T. ground ginger
2 tsp. finely shredded lemon peel
½ tsp. crushed red pepper

1½ lbs. small frozen shrimp, thawed
2 (14-oz.) cans coconut milk
3 T. fresh basil, shredded
4 T. Oriental rice noodles

Bring broth to boiling in a saucepan. Add zucchini, green onion, ginger, lemon grass or lemon peel, and crushed red pepper. Return to boiling; reduce heat. Simmer, uncovered, for 3 minutes, stirring occasionally. Stir in shrimp, and coconut milk. Simmer for a few minutes until hot. Ladle into bowls and top with shredded basil and rice noodles. Serves 4-6.

TUNA SALAD ON RAISIN BREAD

1 lg. can tuna (packed in water) drained well
¼ c. chopped celery
⅛ c. chopped onion
½ c. mayo
1 tsp. prepared mustard
1 pinch garlic salt

1 tsp. sugar
½ tsp. dill
Raisin bread
Thin slices of cucumber
Alfalfa sprouts
Sliced Swiss cheese

Mix tuna, celery, onion, mayo and seasonings together. Spread tuna salad on slice of bread, layer as desired with the rest of the ingredients. Makes 3 sandwiches.

GOURMET GRILLED CHEESE

Spatz bread or deli Italian, sliced
1 slice american cheese
1 slice swiss or mozzarella cheese

Tomato, sliced thin
Bacon slices, cooked

Butter the outside pieces of the bread. Layer the ingredients on the inside. Grill in fry pan, on medium heat until golden brown. Flip over to grill the other side & serve.

Substitution: Your bread choice.

CHICKEN CAESAR WRAP

2 cooked chicken breast, skinless
1/3 c. creamy Caesar salad dressing
2 T. mayo
1 T. grated Parmesan cheese
4 lettuce leaves of your choice
8 thin tomato slices
Onion sliced thin
4 gourmet tortillas of your choice (garden vegetable, wheat, etc)

Slice cooked chicken in thin pieces about 1 inch long. Mix with dressing, mayo and Parmesan cheese. Place a layer of chicken mixture down the center of the wrap. Top with 1 leave of lettuce, a little onion and 2 tomato slices. Roll up and secure with toothpick. Serve cold. Makes 44

SEAFOOD SALAD SANDWICH

1 can shrimp, drained
1 can crabmeat, drained
1/2 c. mayo
1/4 tsp. garlic salt
1/2 tsp. sugar
1 tsp. lemon juice
Pepper to taste
1/2 c. chopped celery
1/4 c. chopped green onion

Mix all ingredients in a bowl. Serve on a Kaiser roll. Add lettuce and tomato if so desired. Makes 4 sandwiches.

ROAST BEEF WRAPS WITH CHEESE SAUCE

1 (16-oz.) jar processed cheese spread
1 tsp. creamy horseradish sauce
2 T. milk
3 med. green onions, sliced
6 tortilla wraps (8 inch diameter)
Mustard
3/4 lb. sliced roast beef (deli style)
Romaine lettuce
Bell pepper strips

First make cheese sauce by heating cheese spread, horseradish sauce and milk until smooth, stirring constantly. Add onions, set aside. Next, spread a scant of mustard on tortilla, top with some roast beef, lettuce and pepper. Roll up and secure with tooth pick. Serve with warm cheese sauce for dipping.

GERMAN HAM SANDWICH

1 T. Dijon mustard
¼ c. apple butter
2 Kaiser rolls, or bread of choice
6 oz. sliced ham

4 oz. Swiss cheese
8 cucumber slices, thin
Lettuce leaves of choice

Mix mustard with apple butter, spread on roll add remaining ingredients. Makes 2 sandwiches.

TURKEY CROISSANT WITH CRANBERRIES

8 oz. softened cream cheese
¼ c. orange marmalade
6 croissants split
1 lb. smoked deli style turkey, sliced

¾ c. whole cranberry sauce
6 leaves of lettuce

Mix cream cheese and marmalade. Spread cheese mixture on both halves of croissants. Layer turkey, cranberries and lettuce on bottom half of croissant. Top with other half and serve. Makes 6 croissants.

CLASSIC FRIED EGG SANDWICH

1 tsp. butter
4 eggs
Miracle whip

4 pcs. bread
Lettuce leaves

Melt butter in fry pan. Fry eggs, break yolks. Spread salad dressing on bread. Top with fried egg and lettuce. Makes 2 sandwiches.

Salads & Vegetables

Helpful Hints

- When preparing a casserole, make an additional batch to freeze. It makes a great emergency meal when unexpected guests arrive. Just take the casserole from the freezer and bake it in the oven.

- To keep hot oil from splattering, sprinkle a little salt or flour in the pan before frying.

- Never overcook foods that are to be frozen. Foods will finish cooking when reheated. Don't refreeze cooked thawed foods.

- A few drops of lemon juice added to simmering rice will keep the grains separated.

- Green pepper may change the flavor of frozen casseroles. Clove, garlic, and pepper flavors get stronger when they are frozen, while sage, onion, and salt get milder.

- Don't freeze cooked egg whites; they become tough.

- For an easy no-mess side dish, grill vegetables along with your meat.

- When freezing foods, label each container with its contents and the date it was put into the freezer. Store at 0°. Always use frozen cooked foods within one to two months.

- Store dried pasta, rice (except brown rice), and whole grains in tightly covered containers in a cool, dry place. Always refrigerate brown rice, and refrigerate or freeze grains if they will not be used within five months.

- To dress up buttered, cooked vegetables, sprinkle them with toasted sesame seeds, toasted chopped nuts, canned french-fried onions, or slightly crushed seasoned croutons.

- Soufflé dishes are designed with straight sides to help your soufflé climb to magnificent heights. Ramekins are good for serving individual casseroles.

- A little vinegar or lemon juice added to potatoes before draining will make them extra white when mashed.

- To quickly bake potatoes, place them in boiling water for 10 to 15 minutes. Pierce their skins with a fork and bake in a preheated oven.

- To avoid toughened beans or corn, add salt midway through cooking.

SALADS & VEGETABLES

9 LAYERED SALAD

1 head lettuce, torn or cut up, or 1 bag of prepared lettuce
1 sm. onion, chopped
5 stalks celery, chopped
1 sm. bag of frozen peas, thawed and dried off with paper towel
6-8 hard-boiled eggs, chopped
1 c. Hellmann's mayonnaise, do not use Miracle whip
1 T. sugar, sprinkle on top of mayo
2 c. shredded cheddar cheese
1 pkg. cooked bacon pieces

In a deep glass bowl, layer in order given, cover with plastic wrap and store in refrigerator for at least 3 hours before serving. Better if made the day before. Serves 8.

MOM'S WILTED SPINACH SALAD

¼ c. chopped, or sliced onion
6 slices cooked crisp bacon, crumble
½ c. cider vinegar
¼ c. water
½ c. sugar
½ tsp. salt
1 tsp. Wondra, or cornstarch
2 hard-boiled eggs, sliced (optional) as garnish
2 bags baby spinach leaves, washed and dried

Cook onions with bacon, drain well. In a small saucepan combine everything but Wondra, eggs and spinach. Heat through while stirring to dissolve sugar. Add Wondra to thicken, stir well. Place spinach in serving bowl, pour dressing over leaves, toss and serve warm. Makes 4 nice size salads.

SANDIE'S BOWTIE CHICKEN PASTA SALAD

½ box bowtie pasta/ make as directed, rinse and drain
3 c. cooked chicken breast, cubed
½ c. chopped celery
½ c. chopped green pepper
½ c. chopped red onion
3 Roma tomatoes, remove seeds, slice
½ c. Hidden Valley ranch dressing
¼ tsp. pepper
¼ tsp. garlic salt

Mix together, chill. Add more ranch dressing if needed. Serves 4-6.

BROCCOLI AND EGG SALAD

2 bunches broccoli
3 hard-boiled eggs, chopped thick
⅓ c. mayonnaise
½ c. sliced green olives
¼ c. chopped onion
2 tsp. lemon juice
¼ tsp. garlic salt

Wash and dry broccoli, using only the flowerets. Cut into bite size pieces. Add the rest of the ingredients, stir well and chill until serving. You may omit the olives, but add 2 tsp. of the juice for the flavor. Serves 4.

CHERRY BROCCOLI SALAD

3 c. broccoli flowerets cut small
½ pkg. cooked bacon, crumbled or 2 oz. cooked real bacon pieces (Hormel)
½ c. dried cherries or dried cranberries
⅓ c. chopped purple onion
⅓ c. salted/roasted sunflower nuts
1 c. mayonnaise
2 T. sugar
2 T. apple cider vinegar

Mix all together in bowl, and chill. Serves 4-6.

LAYERED CAULIFLOWER SALAD

1 head cauliflower, wash, use only flowerets, cut into bite size pieces
1 head lettuce, chopped; or 1 bag plain lettuce
¼ c. chopped purple onion
1 (4-oz.) bag real cooked bacon pieces (Hormel)
1 c. mayonnaise
¼ c. sugar
¼ c. grated Parmesan cheese

Layer the first 4 ingredients in a large salad bowl. Chill. Mix mayo, sugar and cheese for the dressing. Refrigerate. Toss with dressing before serving. Makes 4-6 servings.

ITALIAN MOZZARELLA PASTA SALAD

(3-oz.) cooked angel hair pasta
½ c. chopped celery
4 med. Roma tomatoes, sliced ¼ in. thick
1 c. mozzarella cheese, cubed
1 bag leaf lettuce
1 pkg. prosciutto, cut into bite size pieces
¼ c. chopped fresh basil leaves
¼ c. olive oil
¼ c. red wine vinegar
1 T. sugar
⅛ tsp. Montreal steak seasoning
1 tsp. chopped garlic
⅛ tsp. salt

Break pasta into thirds before cooking as directed, rinse and drain. In a large salad bowl combine pasta with celery, tomatoes, cheese, lettuce and prosciutto. Toss together. Using a salad dressing shaker jar, add the rest of the ingredients. Shake well. Pour onto salad just before serving and toss gently. Serve on individual salad plates.

Substitutions for prosciutto: ham, or pepperoni. Serves 4

SESAME ORANGE ROMAINE SALAD

- 1 lg. can mandarin whole mandarin oranges; drain and reserve juice
- 6 c. bite-size pieces of Romaine lettuce
- 1 c. sliced fresh mushrooms
- 1 c. canned bean sprouts
- ⅓ c. purple onion, sliced thin
- 3 T. seasoned rice vinegar
- 3 T. reserved juice from oranges
- 1 tsp. sesame oil
- 1 T. honey
- ⅛ tsp. cinnamon
- 2 tsp. toasted sesame seeds

Using a large bowl, place oranges, lettuce, mushrooms, sprouts, and onion. Toss. Using a sealed dressing shaker, add the last 6 ingredients together and shake until mixed well. Chill salad and dressing for at least 30 minutes. Shake and pour dressing over salad before serving. Makes 4 salads.

GRILLED CHICKEN SESAME SALAD

- 4 boneless, skinless chicken breast halves
- 1 tsp. Montreal steak seasoning
- 5 c. romaine lettuce, bite size pieces
- ½ seedless cucumber, sliced thin
- ¼ c. sliced thin purple onion
- ¼ c. shredded carrots
- ⅓ c. olive oil
- ¼ c. white vinegar
- ¾ tsp. sugar
- 1 T. toasted sesame seeds
- 1 c. shredded Swiss cheese

Season chicken with a the Montreal steak seasoning. Grill on medium heat for 15 to 20 minutes, or until done. Cut in strips, keep warm. Mix lettuce, cucumbers, onion and carrots in a large bowl. Toss gently. Whisk together, or shake in sealed container the oil, vinegar, sugar, and toasted sesame seeds. Refrigerate until ready to serve. Pour dressing on salad and toss. Serve on individual plates. Top with hot breast of chicken, sprinkle with shredded Swiss cheese. Serves 4.

LAYERED FRUIT & CHEESE SALAD

3 c. fresh peaches- peeled, pitted and sliced
3 c. fresh strawberries, sliced
3 c. green seedless whole grapes
3 c. fresh pears- peeled, cored, and sliced
½ c. Hellmann's canola mayonnaise
½ c. sour cream
1 T. honey
1 ½ c. shredded cheddar cheese

Layer the fruit in a 2-½-quart glass bowl. Mix together mayo, sour cream, and honey. Spread dressing next, then sprinkle on the cheese. Refrigerate until serving. Serves 6-8

PEAS AND PEANUTS

1 c. sour cream
½ tsp. garlic salt
½ tsp. lemon juice
½ T. Worcestershire sauce
1 pkgs. thawed frozen peas
1 can Spanish peanuts

In bowl mix sour cream, garlic salt, lemon juice and Worcestershire sauce. Add peas and peanuts to sour cream mixture, stir together. Cover and refrigerate for at least 3 hours. Serves 4.

ROASTED CHICKEN AND PEAR SALAD

2 bags mixed greens or Romaine lettuce
1½ c. roasted or grilled chicken breast
½ c. Ranch dressing
½ c. chunky bleu cheese dressing
3 pears, cored and sliced
Chinese rice noodles
Ground pepper to taste

In a large bowl combine, greens and chicken. In a small bowl mix the 2 dressings together, pour over greens and chicken. Toss to coat. Using individual salad plates, divide out the salad, top with pear slices and rice noodles. Serves 4.

DRIED CHERRY CHICKEN SALAD

4 c. cooked, skinless chicken breasts
½ c. dried cherries
½ c. diced celery
½ c. diced onion
1½ c. mayonnaise
1½ tsp. dill weed
2 tsp. sugar
Dash of garlic salt
⅓ c. sliced almonds
Lettuce leaves
paprika

Mix everything but the lettuce and paprika together in med. size bowl. Place a lettuce leaf or 2 on a salad plate, add a scoop of chicken salad, garnish with sprinkles of paprika. Serves 4.

MANDARIN ORANGE SALAD WITH ALMONDS

1 bag of Italian lettuce
1 can (15 oz.) mandarin oranges, drained
¼ purple onion, sliced thin and cut in half
1 sm. bag Hormel real bacon
Salt & pepper to taste
¾ c. smoked almonds, whole or cut in halves
Italian shredded cheese
Asian Dressing:
2 T. white wine vinegar
3 T. honey
½ tsp. dry mustard
½ tsp. celery salt
½ tsp. paprika
¼ c. olive oil

Toss together the first 4 ingredients. Mix all the dressing ingredients together in salad shaker or small bowl. Pour Asian dressing on top of salad, toss, serve in salad bowls, and top each with almonds and cheese. Serves 4.

GRILLED CABBAGE

1 head cabbage, quartered and cored
2 strips bacon, uncooked, cut in halves
1 small onion, chopped
½ stick butter, cut in pieces
Garlic salt & pepper to taste

Using a large aluminum-cooking pan, spray with a non-stick butter. Place all ingredients in the pan, sprinkle with the garlic salt and pepper. Cover and grill on low. Stir frequently to prevent burning. Cook until cabbage is soft. Serves 4.

GRILLED MIXED VEGETABLES

2 T. olive oil
1 tsp. chopped garlic
1 T. Worcestershire sauce
¼ c. lemon juice
¼ c. coarse black pepper
1 red pepper, seeded and cubed
1 green pepper, seeded and cubed
1 zucchini, sliced ½ in. thick
1 yellow squash halved lengthwise and slice ½ in. thick
4 green onions, cut in 1 in. pieces
20 snow pea pods
10 mushrooms

Whisk in small bowl, oil, garlic, worcestershire sauce, lemon juice, and pepper. In a separate large bowl combine all of the vegetables. Pour oil mixture over vegetables, stir well. Pour the vegetables into an aluminum foil pan, place on grill. Cook for about 10 minutes, on medium high heat, turn with spoon after 5 minutes of cooking. Serves 4.

GRILLED CORN ON THE COB WITH HERB BUTTER

½ lb. soft butter
1 tsp. chopped parsley, fresh is best
1 tsp. finely chopped chives
dash of garlic salt
6 ears of corn

To make herb butter combine, butter, parsley, chives and garlic salt. Mix well. Set aside. Do not remove husks. Do remove the silk. Soak in water for 20 minutes, remove and pull down husks, without removing totally, spread with the following herbed butter, pull the husks back up covering the corn, using a thin piece of husk, tie at the top of each ear. Place on grill for about 15 minutes, turning 4 times.

GRILLED FRESH GREEN BEANS AND BACON

1 lb. fresh green beans
½ c. sliced sweet onion
¼ c. real bacon pieces
2 T. butter, melted
Garlic salt & pepper to taste

Wash and cut off stems of green beans. Put in large bowl, add the rest of the ingredients and stir. Make an aluminum bag, place beans in bag, double fold seal and grill on a hot grill for about 20 minutes, 10 minutes on each side. Serves 4.

ZUCCHINI GRILL

3 lg. zucchini cut into ½ in. thick slices
3 T. olive oil
2 tsp. oregano
1 tsp. minced garlic
¼ tsp. rosemary
Garlic salt and pepper to taste

Heat grill, brush zucchini with olive oil. Sprinkle both sides with the seasonings. Grill on the rack until tender, about 4 minutes on each side. Serves 4.

MICROWAVE SECRET VEGETABLES

Broccoli
Green beans
Asparagus
Cauliflower

Parsnips, peeled and sliced
Brussel sprouts
Zucchini
Yellow squash

Use any of these fresh vegetables. Place in a 1 or 2 qt. zip lock freezer bag. Add ¼ c. water, seal partially. Microwave for 3 to 5 minutes on high. Some vegetables will need more time. If done to your liking, drain from bag, and add butter and seasonings to taste. Seal, shake, and serve! This keeps them crisp, not over cooked, so all of the nutrients are benefiting YOU.

GRILLED ONION BLOSSOM WITH SAUCE

2 lg. Vidalia onions
½ c. mayo
1 T. ketchup
2 T. creamy horseradish sauce
⅓ tsp. paprika
⅛ tsp. dried basil

Pinch of pepper
⅓ tsp. cayenne pepper
1 tsp. sugar
½ tsp. salt
1 c. crushed garlic croutons

Preheat an outdoor grill for high heat. Peel the onions and cut off ½ inch from the base, so it will sit flat. Slice into 6 to 8 wedges, leaving the base of the onion intact. Pull apart wedges slightly. Mix the rest of the ingredients for the sauce, except the crushed croutons. Spread 1 tablespoon of sauce on each onion, allowing it to drip between layers. Wrap each securely with aluminum foil, double sealing folds, allowing for expansion when heated. Place on grill when hot, med heat, cover grill. Cook for 15 to 20 min. Remove from grill, open carefully allowing steam to escape. Sprinkle each with crushed croutons. Return opened packets to grill, cover and cook for 8 to 10 min. longer, or until onions are tender and lightly browned. Serve with remaining sauce. Serves 4.

GRILLED PARMESAN POTATOES

3 med. russet potatoes
3 T. Parmesan cheese, grated
2 tsp. olive oil

¼ tsp. Italian seasoning
¼ tsp. garlic salt
¼ tsp. onion powder

Preheat grill. Cut unpeeled potatoes into 8 equal pieces, place in center of aluminum foil. Combine other ingredients except cheese in a small bowl, and then drizzle over potatoes. Toss lightly. Fold foil over potatoes and seal. Place on hot grill for 30 to 40 min. Potatoes should pierce easily with fork, if so, add cheese and return to grill for 5 minutes or until cheese has melted. Serves 4.

GRILLED, TWICE BAKED POTATOES

3 lg. baking potatoes
1½ c. shredded cheddar cheese
¼ c. chopped green onion
½ c. sour cream

½ tsp. garlic salt
Chopped tomatoes, or red pepper
¼ tsp. pepper
Fresh ground pepper to taste

Prick potatoes with fork several times, place on paper towels in microwave. Cook on high for 10 to 15 min. turning potatoes several times, until almost tender. Let stand 10 minutes to cool. Cut potatoes in half, lengthwise. Using a spoon scoop out pulp from each half, leaving a small layer in the bottom. Chop potato pulp, place in lg. bowl. Add cheese, onions, sour cream and salt. Mix lightly. Stir in tomatoes or red pepper. Spoon into potato shells: sprinkle with pepper. Place potatoes on med. heated grill, close or cover with foil. Cook 10 to 12 minutes or until cheese has melted. Serves 6.

SMOKEY CHEDDAR POTATOES

4 med. med. potatoes, cut in chunks, unpeeled
½ tsp. salt
2 T. butter melted
1 c. shredded cheddar cheese
2 T. cooked real bacon pieces (Hormel)
2 green onions, sliced
1 tsp. fresh chopped basil or parsley

Place cut potatoes in a large bowl. Add the rest of the ingredients and mix. Place on a large sheet of heavy-duty foil. Wrap securely. Poke with fork once or twice to vent. Grill packet seam side up, for 45 to 60 minutes, or until potatoes are tender. You may pre-microwave in a microwave safe bowl for 10 minutes to speed up cooking process. Makes 4 servings.

OLD FASHION GERMAN POTATO SALAD

9 potatoes
1 lb. bacon
1 c. chopped onion
1 c. chopped celery
3 T. flour
1⅓ c. water
⅔ c. cider vinegar
⅔ c. sugar
2 tsp. salt
½ tsp. pepper

Cook potatoes in boiling salted water until tender but firm. Cool, peel and cut into cubes. Cook bacon; drain fat reserving ¼ c. Cook the onion and celery in the ¼ c. reserved fat for 1 minute. Blend flour and water in a cup; add this and the vinegar to celery and onions. Stir constantly while cooking, until thick and bubbly. Stir in sugar, salt, pepper. Add dressing to potatoes; toss lightly. Simmer on very low for 45 minutes; stir frequently. Serve hot. Makes 6 servings.

Recipe Favorites

Poultry, Beef & Pork

78776-sg-5m

Helpful Hints

- Use little oil when preparing sauces and marinades for red meats. Fat from the meat will render out during cooking and will provide plenty of flavor. Certain meats, like ribs and pot roast, can be par-boiled before grilling to reduce the fat content.

- When trying to reduce your fat intake, buy the leanest cuts you can find. Fat will show up as an opaque white coating or can also run through the meat fibers, as marbling. Although most of the fat (the white coating) can be trimmed away, there isn't much that can be done about the marbling. Stay away from well-marbled cuts of meat.

- Home from work late with no time for marinating meat? Pound meat lightly with a mallet or rolling pin, pierce with a fork, sprinkle lightly with meat tenderizer, and add marinade. Refrigerate for about 20 minutes, and you'll have succulent, tender meat.

- Marinating is a cinch if you use a plastic bag. The meat stays in the marinade and it's easy to turn and rearrange. Cleanup is easy; just toss the bag.

- It's easier to thinly slice meat if it's partially frozen.

- Tomatoes added to roasts will help to naturally tenderize them. Tomatoes contain an acid that works well to break down meats.

- Whenever possible, cut meats across the grain; they will be easier to eat and have a better appearance.

- When frying meat, sprinkle paprika over it to turn it golden brown.

- Thaw all meats in the refrigerator for maximum safety.

- Refrigerate poultry promptly after purchasing. Keep it in the coldest section of your refrigerator for up to two days. Freeze poultry for longer storage. Never leave poultry at room temperature for more than two hours.

- If you're microwaving skinned chicken, cover the baking dish with vented clear plastic wrap to keep the chicken moist.

- Lemon juice rubbed on fish before cooking will enhance the flavor and help maintain a good color.

- Scaling a fish is easier if vinegar is rubbed on the scales first.

78776-sg-5m

POULTRY, BEEF & PORK

BREAST OF CHICKEN WITH GREEN ONION SAUCE

3 T. butter
4 boneless chicken breasts
2 green onions, chopped
3 T. fresh chopped basil
1 T. fresh chopped parsley
¼ c. dry white wine
1 c. chicken broth, heated
1 tsp. brown sugar
1 T. Wondra
3 T. hot water
Juice of 1 lime
½ tsp. Montreal steak seasoning

Heat half of the butter in a fry pan over medium heat. Add chicken, season with steak seasoning and cook for 5 minutes on each side. Remove from stove and set aside. Do not drain. Chop green onion using some of the greens. Heat remaining butter in sauté pan over medium heat. Add green onions, basil, parsley and wine. Cover and cook for 3 minutes. Stir in chicken broth, brown sugar, and lime juice. Cook another 6 minutes over low heat. Dissolve Wondra in the hot water, stir into sauce and bring to a boil. Cook 1 minute. Return fry pan with chicken to the stove, pour the sauce over the chicken and simmer for about 10- 15 minutes. Serve the chicken with the sauce on cooked fettuccini. Serves 4.

GARLIC CHICKEN

4 boneless chicken breasts
3 T. canola oil
1 envelope garlic mushroom soup mix

Toss together in a sealed freezer bag. Grill or broil until done and chicken is no longer pink. Makes 4 servings.

APPLE SAUCE GRILLED CHICKEN

1 med. onion, chopped fine
2 T. canola oil
1 c. granny smith applesauce
1 c. ketchup
¼ c. cider vinegar
2 T. brown sugar
1 T. Worcestershire sauce
1 whole chicken, cut up/ or 4 chicken breasts

    Sauté onion in oil until soft. Add the rest of ingredients, except the chicken. Bring to boil while stirring. Reduce heat and let simmer. Remove when thickened. Place chicken on hot grill. Cook each side for 12 minutes. Brush a heavy layer of sauce on the chicken. While cooking, continue to brush on sauce until chicken is done. Serves 4.

SIMPLY YUMMY TERIYAKI CHICKEN

1 c. Hellmann's mayo
¾ c. soy sauce
4 chicken breasts

    Whip the mayo and soy together. Place chicken in a shallow dish, pour ½ of the marinate over the chicken, coat well. Reserve the other ½. Refrigerate up to 4 hours. Remove chicken from dish, place on hot grill and discard that marinate. Cook chicken about 10 to 15 minutes on each side and brush on the reserved marinate while cooking. Serves 4.

SESAME GRILLED CHICKEN

2 lg. chicken breasts with skin
⅓ c. soy sauce
2 T. brown sugar
1 tsp. minced garlic, or 2 cloves chopped
1 T. sesame seeds

    Place chicken breasts in a plastic food bag that you can seal. Mix soy, sugar, and garlic in a cup, then pour over the chicken in the bag, toss to coat. Refrigerate for at least 4 hours. Occasionally, turn the bag of chicken to coat well with sauce. Remove chicken from bag. Discard marinade. Place chicken on hot grill, skin side up. Sprinkle sesame seeds on top. Cook 30 to 40 minutes, turning twice, or until chicken is tender and done. Serves 2.

ORANGE GINGER CHICKEN

½ c. olive oil
2 T. grated ginger
1 tsp. minced garlic, or 2 cloves minced
3 lbs. chicken pieces
¼ tsp. salt
¼ pepper
½ c. orange marmalade
2 T. orange juice

Combine oil, ginger and garlic. Mix well. Brush over chicken pieces, sprinkle with salt and pepper. Let stand 15 minutes at room temp. Combine marmalade and orange juice. Preheat grill to medium. Place chicken on grill and cook for about 30 minutes. During the last 15 minutes of cooking, brush on marmalade and juice mixture. Turn often. Serves 4.

SOUR CREAM BURGERS

2 lbs. ground chuck
1 envelope dry onion soup mix
1 c. sour cream
½ c. seasoned bread crumbs
Pepper to taste

Mix all together in a large bowl. Make patties. Grill or cook in fry pan until done to your liking. Serves 6.

THE SPECIAL GRILLED BURGER

1 lb. ground beef
¼ tsp. salt & pepper
¼ tsp. minced garlic
2 T. finely chopped onion
1 T. A-1 steak sauce
2 T. ketchup
1 T. Worcestershire sauce
1 T. cooking oil
1 tsp. vinegar
3 drops of hot pepper sauce, if desired.

Combine ground beef, salt and pepper. Make into ¾ inch patties. Should make 4 of them. Grill on medium heat for 15 to 20 minutes, turning once. In a sauce pan combine the rest of the ingredients. Bring to boil, reduce heat and simmer uncovered for 5 minutes. Remove from heat and set aside. Brush sauce on burgers frequently and generously while grilling during the last 5 minutes. Serve on a bun with your choice of condiments. Serves 4.

BBQ SLOPPY JOES

1 lb. ground beef
6 hamburger buns
½ c. chopped onion
½ c. chopped celery
1 clove garlic, chopped
¼ c. chili sauce
1 c. water
1 tsp. salt
¼ tsp. pepper
1 T. Worcestershire sauce
2 T. vinegar
2 T. brown sugar
1 tsp. dry mustard
½ tsp. paprika
½ tsp. chili powder
1 tsp. parsley

Brown ground beef and drain. Place in 2 qt. saucepan. Add the rest of the ingredients, stir, simmer for 30 minutes, stirring occasionally. Serves 4-6.

GRILLED BEEF FAJITAS

½ lb. boneless steak, cut into bite size strips
½ lg. onion sliced ½ in. thick
1 lg. green pepper, cut into thin bite size strips
2 T. fajita seasoning
4 Flour tortillas, 8 in. size
2 T. lime juice
4 T. salsa
4 T. sour cream

Combine steak pieces, onions, green pepper and fajita seasoning in plastic bag, shake to coat. On a heated grill, place steak and vegetables on bottom rack, close to heat. Cook 4 to 6 minutes. Heat tortillas on top rack to warm. When done, transfer to plate and sprinkle with lime juice. Spoon steak and vegetables down the center of the tortilla. Top with 1 T. each of salsa and sour cream. Fold up sides of tortilla to cover filling, press together to seal. Makes 4 Fajitas.

MARINATED STEAK

2 tsp. mashed garlic, or 4 cloves
3 T. olive oil
3 T. teriyaki sauce
3 drops of sesame oil

¼ c. lemon juice
Fresh ground pepper to taste
4 steaks of your choice

Put all ingredients except steaks in a bowl and mix. Place steaks in a shallow dish, spread with marinade. Cover and put in refrigerator for 3 hours before cooking. Grill steaks as desired, discard marinade. Serves 4.

CORNED BEEF BRISKET DINNER/ WITH SAUCE

1½ lb. corned beef brisket with seasoning
5 whole bay leaves
½ tsp. thyme
5 medium size white potatoes (peeled and halved)
8 carrots (peeled)

1 head cabbage (quartered)
Salt, pepper, to taste
Butter, to taste
½ c. Hellmann's mayo
¼ c. Marzetti's Southwest Caesar Dressing
1 tsp. sugar

Place brisket in slow cooker, fat side down. Add water enough to cover the brisket. Add the bay leaves and thyme. Cover and cook on high for 2 hours, turn to low, let cook another 5 hours. Now add potatoes, carrots and cabbage, in that order, cabbage on top to steam. Allow to cook another 2 hours or more on low. When potatoes and carrots are tender, it is done. Remove the brisket, trim off the fat from the bottom before you cut and serve with the vegetables. Salt, pepper and butter potatoes, cabbage and carrots. Serve sauce on the side, or a dollop on each individual serving of corned beef. Sauce: Mix together mayo, Caesar dressing and sugar. May make ahead and just store in refrigerator. Serves 4.

GRILLED PORK CHOPS WITH PESTO

4 lg. boneless pork chops
Cooking spray
4 T. pesto
3 T. plain bread crumbs

Spray each side of pork chop with cooking spray. Place pork chops on heated grill, near the bottom. Cook 5 minutes on each side, or until done. Spread ½ T. of pesto, sprinkle bread crumbs on each chop. Continue cooking until pork is no longer pink. Serve with a ½ T. pesto on top. Serves 4.

GRILLED PORK TENDERLOIN WITH MANGO SALSA

1 lb. pork tenderloin cut into ½ inch thick slices
1½ tsp. Jamaican or Caribbean jerk seasoning
1 med. med. mango peeled and cubed
1 jalapeño chile, chopped fine and seeded
2 T. chopped fresh cilantro
1 T. lime juice
1 T. honey

Sprinkle both sides of pork slices with seasoning. Mix the rest of the ingredients together in bowl, cover and refrigerate until almost ready to serve. On a heated grill, place pork on bottom rack. Close grill and cook 8 to 10 minutes or until no longer pink. Heat mango salsa. Remove from grill, spoon mango salsa on top of pork chop. Yummy! Makes 4 servings.

SNAPPY BBQ PORK CHOPS

1 onion, chopped fine
2 tsp. minced garlic
4 T. butter
1 c. dry white wine
2 T. brown sugar
1 c. tomato sauce
½ c. ketchup
1 T. horseradish
2 tsp. dry mustard
2 T. chili powder
½ tsp. pepper
1 tsp. celery salt
6 (¾ in. thick) pork chops

Sauté onion and garlic in butter, pour in wine, and cook 2 minutes over high heat. Add remaining ingredients, and bring to a boil. Cook 15 minutes over low heat. Mix all ingredients except pork chops together. Brush sauce onto pork chops and marinate for 15 minutes. When grill is hot, spray a non-stick cooking spray on rack. Place chops on grill. Cook 8 to 10 minutes, basting 4 to 5 times with sauce. Serves 6.

ZESTY GRILLED PORK CHOPS

2 c. Zesty Italian dressing
¼ c. soy sauce
½ tsp. steak seasoning
4 boneless pork chops

Preheat grill to medium heat. Mix the dressing, soy and seasoning in a small bowl. Place pork chops in a shallow foil pan. Pour the dressing over the top of the pork chops, cover and cook for about 25 minutes, turning a few times. Remove cover, reduce heat to low and continue to cook to desired doneness. This may be done on the stove or electric fry pan. Serves 4.

GRILLED ITALIAN SAUSAGE

1 tsp. mashed garlic
2 T. teriyaki sauce
1 T. olive oil
2 T. ketchup
¼ c. lemon juice
3 drops hot pepper sauce or Tabasco
fresh ground pepper to taste
4 large spicy Italian sausage

Mix all ingredients together in a small bowl except sausage. Place sausage on a platter and pour sauce over top. Cover and let stand 15 minutes, turning sausages 3 times. Oil grill with spray, cook sausages covered on med. high for 5 minutes on each side. Serves 4.

GRILLED PESTO STEAK WITH BLEU CHEESE SAUCE

2 steaks of choice
Salt & ground pepper
1 c. jarred pesto
1 T. unsalted butter
½ tsp. minced garlic

¾ tsp. fresh thyme, chopped
1 c. heavy cream
¼ lb. crumbled bleu cheese
⅛ tsp. Montreal steak seasoning

Season steak with salt and pepper. Brush the pesto onto both sides of the steak. Grill to your likeness. While the steaks are cooking, sauté butter, garlic and thyme, over medium-low heat for 2 minutes. Do not let the garlic turn brown. Add cream, simmer over medium heat until cream reduces by ⅓. Lower heat to a slow simmer. Stir in cheese until melted and smooth. Add steak seasoning. Ladle over steak. Serves 2. This sauce can also be put into a fondue pot for dipping pieces of steak on a skewer.

Recipe Favorites

Fish
& Seafood

Helpful Hints

- To refinish antiques or revitalize wood, use equal parts of linseed oil, white vinegar, and turpentine. Rub into the furniture or wood with a soft cloth and lots of elbow grease.

- To stop the ants in your pantry, seal off cracks where they are entering with putty or petroleum jelly. Also, try sprinkling red pepper on floors and counter tops.

- To fix sticking sliding doors, windows, and drawers, rub wax along their tracks.

- To make a simple polish for copper bottom cookware, mix equal parts of flour and salt with vinegar to create a paste. Store the paste in the refrigerator.

- Applying baking soda on a damp sponge will remove starch deposits from an iron. Make sure the iron is cold and unplugged.

- Remove stale odors in the wash by adding baking soda.

- To clean Teflon™, combine 1 cup water, 2 tablespoons baking soda and ½ cup liquid bleach. Boil in stained pan for 5 to 10 minutes or until the stain disappears. Wash, rinse, dry, and condition with oil before using the pan again.

- Corning Ware can be cleaned by filling it with water and dropping in two denture cleaning tablets. Let stand for 30 to 45 minutes.

- A little instant coffee will work wonders on your wood furniture. Just make a thick paste from instant coffee and a little water, and rub it into the nicks and scratches on your dark wood furniture. You'll be amazed at how new and beautiful those pieces will look.

- For a clogged shower head, boil it for 15 minutes in a mixture of ½ cup vinegar and 1 quart water.

- For a spicy aroma, toss dried orange or lemon rinds into the fireplace.

- Add raw rice to the salt shaker to keep the salt free-flowing.

- Ice cubes will help sharpen garbage disposal blades.

- Separate stuck-together glasses by filling the inside one with cold water and setting them in hot water.

FISH & SEAFOOD

HONEY MUSTARD SALMON

2 T. olive oil
2 salmon filets
dash garlic salt
dash Montreal steak seasoning

2 T. honey
2 T. water
2 tsp. soy sauce
1 tsp. dry mustard

Preheat grill to medium high. Brush oil on salmon, sprinkle with garlic salt and Montreal steak seasoning. Mix the honey, water, soy sauce and mustard together. Place salmon on foil. Brush both sides of salmon with glaze while grilling. Cook for 10 minutes on one side, flip and cook another 8 to 10 minutes, or until flakey. Serves 2.

GRILLED WHISKEY TUNA STEAKS

1/3 c. Teriyaki sauce
1/3 c. soy sauce
1 tsp. minced garlic
Juice of 1/2 lemon

1 1/2 T. whiskey
1 tsp. liquid smoke, if desired
2 Tuna steaks (1 inch thick)

Mix everything together in small bowl, except the tuna. Place steaks in marinade, cover and let stand 15 minutes. Discard marinade. Cook steaks on pre-heated grill for about 20 minutes. Steaks should be pink in the center. You may substitute the tuna with salmon also. Serves 2.

BLACKENED GROUPER, WHITEFISH, OR COD

1 tsp. black pepper	1 tsp. paprika
1 tsp. chili powder	1 tsp. cayenne pepper
1 tsp. thyme	½ c. olive oil
½ tsp. ginger	4 fish filets of your choice

Preheat grill to medium high. Mix all of the dry seasonings together in a small bowl. Using some of the olive oil, brush the filets well. Pour the rest of the oil into a 9x13 aluminum foil pan, spreading it evenly. Place pan on heated grill, when hot add mixed spices to the oil and cook 2 minutes, stirring occasionally. Add fish to pan, reduce heat to medium and cook 3 minutes on each side. Turn grill down to low and continue cooking for about 8 to 10 minutes. Serve with lemon or tartar sauce. Makes 4 servings.

SALMON FILETS WITH HOME MADE LEMON BUTTER

4 T. melted butter	4 T. paprika
4 salmon filets	2 T. dried mustard
1 c. flour	½ tsp. sweet basil
2 T. garlic salt	½ tsp. thyme

Brush the melted butter generously on both sides of filets. Mix the rest of the ingredients together in a small bowl. Pre-heat grill to medium high. Dredge both sides of filets in the flour mixture. Place a piece of aluminum foil on grill and spray with a non-stick oil. Grill fish on the foil for about 7 minutes on each side. Cooking time will depend upon how hot the grill is. Serve hot with my homemade lemon butter.

LEMON BUTTER FOR FISH

½ lb. softened butter
2 T. parsley
1 T. chives, chopped fine
¼ c. lemon juice

3 drops of Worcestershire sauce
2 drops of Tabasco sauce
Salt and pepper to taste

Blend everything together. Spoon butter onto a piece of foil down the center, make into a cylinder shape. Twist ends shut. Refrigerate to set. Slice the butter and place one slice on each cooked piece of fish before serving. Garnish with fresh dill or parsley.

HUBBY'S SUPER FRIED WALLEYE OR PERCH

1½ c. Hungry Jack buttermilk
  pancake mix
1 T. Lawry's seasoning salt
1 T. Lawry's seasoned pepper

1 c. milk
¼ c. vegetable oil
1 lb. walleye or perch; skinned
  and cut into fillets

Mix in bowl, pancake mix and seasonings. Pour milk into a shallow small bowl, dip fish in milk, shaking off excess. Dredge filets in flour mixture until well coated and covered completely. Using an iron skillet on the grill, pour in oil and allow it to get hot. To test temp, drop a pinch of flour mixture in and it should sizzle. Place fish in hot oil, fry until flaky and golden brown. Serve with lemon butter, tarter sauce, or lemon. This may be done on the stove also. Everyone loves fish done this way. Serves 2-4.

SAUTÉED SHRIMP WITH VEGETABLES

1 lb. uncooked shrimp, peeled
  and deveined
1 tsp. minced garlic
2 T. teriyaki
2 T. olive oil
1 pinch of crushed chilies

1 small onion, chopped large
1 lg. zucchini sliced with skin, or
  broccoli flowerets
¼ c. lemon juice, or juice of 1
  lemon
1 tsp. garlic salt

Mix everything together in a large bowl: Place in a foil bag or make one with a large piece of foil. Preheat grill. Cook about 8 minutes or until shrimp is pink. Turn once while cooking. Serve with rice or pasta. Makes 3 to 4 servings.

SHRIMP AND SCALLOP SKEWERS WITH DIPPING SAUCE

2 T. peanut oil
2 jalapeño chilies, minced
½ tsp. ginger
½ tsp. garlic, minced
¾ c. dry white wine
⅓ c. soy sauce
⅓ c. dark brown sugar

2 tsp. Wondra
1 T. lime juice
¼ c. fresh cilantro
24 lg. raw shrimp, peeled and deveined
24 lg. raw sea scallops

Heat oil in small saucepan, over low heat. Stir in chilies, ginger and garlic. Cover, and heat for 6 minutes. Stir occasionally. Combine, wine, soy, brown sugar, and Wondra to the chilies mixture. Stir until Wondra is dissolved. Cook on medium-high heat, continue to stir until it comes to a boil. Should thicken. Pour into a bowl and set aside to cool, and then add lime juice. Remove ½ cup of sauce; put in another bowl and add the cilantro. Reserve that ½ for serving. Tread shrimp and scallops onto skewers. Using the other half of sauce, brush the scallops and shrimp and place on preheated grill. Cook for about 3 minutes, or until done. Remove from grill and serve with remaining sauce. Makes 8 skewers.

EASY SHRIMP SCAMPI

2 lbs. raw large shrimp, peeled, deveined
6 T. butter
2 T. chopped onion
1 T. minced garlic, or freshly chopped

1 T. fresh squeezed lemon juice
2 tsp. fresh dill weed, chopped
¼ c. fresh snipped parsley

Rinse shrimp well in water. Pat dry with paper towel. Melt butter in skillet until sizzling, add onions and garlic. Cook for 2 to 3 minutes. Add shrimp, cook until pink. Stir in the rest of the ingredients and cook for about 3 minutes more. Serve over pasta. Makes 6 servings.

Sauces, Marinades & Dressings

Helpful Hints

- Push animal shaped cookie cutters lightly into icing on cakes or cupcakes. Fill depressed outlines with chocolate icing or decorating confections.

- Fill flat bottomed ice cream cones half full with cake batter and bake. Top with icing and decorating confections.

- To make cookie crumbs for your recipes, put cookies into a plastic bag and run a rolling pin back and forth until they are the right size.

- To decorate cookies with chocolate, place cookies on a rack over waxed paper. Dip the tines of a fork with chocolate, and wave the fork gently back and forth making wavy lines.

- A gadget that works well for decorating sugar cookies is an empty plastic thread spool. Simply press the spool into the dough, imprinting a pretty flower design.

- Some holiday cookies require an indent on top to fill with jam or chocolate. Use the rounded end of a honey dipper to make the indent.

- Tin coffee cans make excellent freezer containers for cookies.

- If you only have one cookie sheet on hand, line it with parchment paper. While one batch is baking, load a second sheet of parchment paper to have another batch ready to bake. Cleaning is also easier.

- When a recipe calls for packed brown sugar, fill the correct size measuring cup with the sugar, and then use the next smaller size cup to pack the brown sugar into its cup.

- Dipping strawberries in chocolate? Stick toothpicks into the stem end of the berry. Coat the berries with chocolate, shaking off any excess. Turn the berries upside down and stick the toothpick into a block of styrofoam until the chocolate is set. The finished berries will have chocolate with no flat spots. Another easy solution is to place dipped berries dipped-side up in the holes of an egg carton.

- Cut-up dried fruit sometimes sticks to the blade of your knife. To prevent this problem, coat the blade of your knife with a thin film of vegetable spray before cutting.

- Cutting dessert bars is easier if you score the bars as soon as the pan comes out of the oven. When the bars cool, cut along the scored lines.

SAUCES, MARINADES & DRESSINGS

SANDIE'S RED WINE VINEGAR SALAD DRESSING

1 c. extra virgin olive oil
¼ c. red wine vinegar
2 T. water
½ tsp. minced garlic
¼ tsp. Montreal steak seasoning
½ tsp. dill weed
½ pkg. dry Italian dressing mix

Using a salad dressing shaker, add all of the ingredients, shake and refrigerate for at least 3 hours. Shake before serving. You may also use the lines on the shaker for the oil, vinegar and water, then add seasonings. This makes a very healthy and tasty dressing for any salad. Serves 6-8.

TARTAR SAUCE

1 c. mayo, not salad dressing
1½ T. sweet pickle relish
1 tsp. creamy horseradish sauce

Mix together and refrigerate. Serves 4.

DILL HOLLANDAISE SAUCE FOR GRILLED SALMON

1 pkg. Hollandaise sauce mix
½ tsp. lemon juice
2 T. fresh-chopped dill, or 1 teaspoon dried dill

Prepare Hollandaise sauce as directed on pkg. Stir in lemon juice and dill. Ladle over salmon. Serves 4.

CUCUMBER DILL SAUCE

1½ c. Hidden Valley ranch dressing
1 tsp. dried dill, or 2 tsp. fresh-chopped dill
1 tsp. sugar
¼ c. seedless cucumber, finely chopped
3 T. finely chopped onion
⅛ tsp. garlic salt
1 tsp. parsley
1 T. orange juice

Mix all ingredients together, refrigerate until serving. This is great for salmon and also vegetables. Serves 6.

NEW TWIST TARTER SAUCE

¾ c. Hellmann's Canola Mayonnaise
¼ c. Jacks Special Salsa, drained
½ tsp. sugar
½ tsp. dill weed

Mix all ingredients together in a small bowl. Refrigerate for at least 3 hours before serving with the fish of your choice. Serves 4-6.

MUSHROOM SAUCE

2 T. butter
1 T. olive oil
12 mushrooms, thinly sliced
2 T. flour
¼ tsp. fresh thyme
Salt & pepper to taste
¼ c. green onion, chopped
3 c. chicken broth

In small saucepan, melt butter with the oil over medium heat. Add mushrooms, cook until dark and tender. Add salt, pepper and thyme and green onion. Sprinkle flour over the mushrooms, stir, and cook for 1 minute. Whisk in the broth and cook 5 minutes over med-low heat until thickened. Serve over your choice of meat, pasta or potatoes. Serves 6.

SWEET AND SOUR SAUCE FOR CHICKEN OR MEATBALLS

6 T. soy sauce
2 garlic clove, pressed, or 1 tsp. minced garlic
1½ c. plum preserves
½ c. chili sauce
¼ tsp. ground ginger

Mix together and heat. Great for meatballs in a crock-pot, basted on grilled chicken, or served as a sauce to dip chicken skewers, nuggets, etc.

SALMON GLAZE

3 T. butter
¾ c. brown sugar
2¼ tsp. lemon juice
1 tsp. dill weed
⅛ tsp. lemon pepper

Melt everything together, and brush on salmon many times while grilling.

SALMON GLAZE II

4 T. butter, melted
½ c. brown sugar
⅓ c. whiskey

Mix together, brush on to salmon while grilling.

BBQ WHISKEY SAUCE

3 T. butter
1 med. onion, chopped
2 garlic cloves, mashed
4 T. flour
3 c. beef broth, heated
¼ c. vinegar
1 (5-oz.) can tomato paste
¼ c. brown sugar
Salt & pepper to taste
3 T. whiskey

In sauce pan heat butter on medium heat. Add onions and garlic, cook for about 6 minutes. Add flour, mix well and cook over low heat for 5 minutes more. Add broth, vinegar, tomato paste and brown sugar. Stir well, season with salt and pepper, and add the whiskey. Cook for about 15 minutes over low heat. Place your choice of chicken, ribs or pork on foil. Ladle sauce over the top, and cover with the foil. Grill for 45 minutes or until done, turning a few times during the cooking process. Serves 4.

MARINATE FOR GRILLED FISH

½ c. sliced sweet onions
¼ c. olive oil
2 T. orange juice
2 T. lime juice
2 T. fresh cilantro, chopped
2 tsp. minced garlic
1 tsp. salt
1 tsp. cumin
Pinch of pepper

Combine all ingredients into a bowl. Stir well. Pour over fish, cover and refrigerate for at least 1 hour or more. When ready to grill, remove fish, and discard the marinate. Cook fish as desired. Makes 4 servings.

PORK LOIN GLAZE

1½ c. apple juice
1 T. fresh rosemary, chopped fine
¼ c. brown sugar
2 T. Wondra
2 T. cold water

In saucepan combine apple juice, chopped rosemary and sugar. In a mixing cup mix Wondra and cold water together. Bring apple juice mixture to a boil and whisk in the Wondra mixture to thicken and remove from heat. Spoon glaze over sliced pork loin to finish it off with perfection!

Desserts

Helpful Hints

- Egg whites need to be at room temperature for greater volume when whipped. Remember this when making meringue.

- When preparing several batches of pie dough, roll dough out between sheets of plastic wrap. Stack the discs in a pizza box, and keep the box in the freezer. Pull out the required crusts as needed.

- Place your pie plate on a cake stand when placing the pie dough in it and fluting the edges. The cake stand will make it easier to turn the pie plate, and you won't have to stoop over.

- Many kitchen utensils can be used to make decorative pie edges. For a scalloped edge, use a spoon. Crosshatched and herringbone patterns are achieved with a fork. For a sharply pointed effect, use a can opener to cut out points around the rim.

- Keep strawberries fresh for up to ten days by refrigerating them (unwashed) in an airtight container between layers of paper towels.

- When grating citrus peel, bits of peel are often stuck in the holes of the grater. Rather than waste the peel, you can easily brush it off by using a new, clean toothbrush.

- To core a pear, slice the pear in half lengthwise. Use a melon baller to cut out the central core, using a circular motion. Draw the melon baller to the top of the pear, removing the interior stem as you go.

- When cutting butter into flour for pastry dough, the process is easier if you cut the butter into small pieces before adding it to the flour.

- To keep the cake plate clean while frosting, slide 6-inch strips of waxed paper under each side of the cake. Once the cake is frosted and the frosting is set, pull the strips away leaving a clean plate.

- When decorating a cake with chocolate, you can make a quick decorating tube. Put chocolate in a heat-safe zipper-lock plastic bag. Immerse in simmering water until the chocolate is melted. Snip off the tip of one corner, and squeeze the chocolate out of the bag.

- Professionally decorated cakes have a silky, molten look. To get that appearance, frost your cake as usual, then use a hair dryer to blow-dry the surface until the frosting slightly melts.

- To ensure that you have equal amounts of batter in each pan when making a layered cake, use a kitchen scale to measure the weight.

DESSERTS

PEANUT BUTTER CANDY BARS

1½ c. margarine, melted
2 c. peanut butter
½ tsp. vanilla
4½ c. powdered sugar

2 c. graham cracker crumbs
½ c. melted butter
2 c. semi sweet chocolate chips

Combine the first 5 ingredients and mix. Spread in the bottom of a greased 10 x 15 pan. Place butter and chips in a micro-wavable bowl and cook for 45 seconds. Stir, cook another few seconds or until melted. Stir until smooth. Spread over peanut butter mixture. Let cool completely. Cut into bars.

POPCORN BARS

12 c. popped popcorn
1 c. semi sweet chocolate chips
1 c. salted peanuts

½ c. butter, melted
½ c. cup creamy peanut butter
4½ c. miniature marshmallows

In a very large bowl, combine popped corn, chocolate chips and peanuts. Mix well. In a medium saucepan add butter, peanut butter, and marshmallows. Stir over low heat until melted. Add marshmallow mixture to the popcorn mixture, stir together until coated well. Press into greased 9x13 pan. Allow to cool before cutting into squares.

CHOCOLATE DIPPED FRUIT

1½ c. semi sweet chocolate chips
½ c. white chocolate chips
½ c. milk chocolate chips
3 T. butter
Fresh cut pineapple chunks
Strawberries
Dried apricots
Banana slices
Fresh pear slices
Shortbread cookies

    Using a medium bowl, mix then microwave first 4 ingredients on full power for 1- 2 minutes, or until melted. Stir well until smooth. Using a small fondue pot, place chocolate inside to keep it melted. Use mini skewers to dip in your favorite fruits. Cookies may be dipped by hand and eaten, or cover half with chocolate and place on wax paper until set. Serves 4-6.

HEAVENLY PUDDING CAKE

1 (10-oz.) prepared angel food cake
1 sm. pkg. instant choc pudding
1 sm. pkg. instant vanilla pudding
6 c. cold milk, for puddings
2 (2-oz.) bars Butterfingers, crushed
Whipped cream topping

    Cube the angel food cake, place ½ in the bottom of a 9x13 pan or dish. Prepare the 2 puddings as directed on pkg. Spread the chocolate pudding on the top of the cake cubes in pan. Top then with ½ of the crushed candy. Layer the rest of cubed cake evenly. Top with the vanilla pudding, whipped topping, and remaining candy. Chill until serving. Serves 8-10.

ELEGANT CHERRY OR BLUEBERRY TORTE

1 (14-oz.) prepared pound cake
1½ c. prepared vanilla pudding
1 (12-oz.) can of cherry or blueberry pie filling
(12-oz.) whipped topping
½ c. chopped nuts, or mini semi sweet chocolate chips

    Slice cake horizontally into 3 layers. Place one layer on a serving dish, top with vanilla pudding. Add 2nd slice of cake, top with pie filling. Add 3rd and final piece of cake, spread with whipped topping. Sprinkle chopped nuts or semi sweet mini chocolate chips. Chill well. Slice and serve. Makes 6 slices.

CHOCOLATE OAT BARS

1 c. butter
½ c. brown sugar
1 tsp. vanilla
3 c. uncooked quick oats

1 c. semi-sweet chocolate chips
½ c. crunchy or creamy peanut butter

Grease a 9-inch square pan. Melt butter over med heat in saucepan. Add brown sugar and vanilla; stir until smooth. Stir in quick oats; cook 2 to 3 minutes over low heat, until well blended. Press ½ of mixture into pan, spread evenly. Melt chocolate chips in microwavable bowl for about 1 minute, or until melted. Stir until smooth. Pour this over oat mixture. Spread with knife. Crumble remaining oat mixture over chocolate layer; press down gently. Cover and refrigerate for 3 hours or overnight. Let thaw 10 minutes before cutting into 1-inch bars. These may be frozen. Serves 6.

PEANUT BUTTER CREAM PIE

⅓ c. creamy peanut butter
¾ c. powdered sugar
1 baked (9 inch) pie crust
1 c. milk
1 c. sour cream

1 sm. pkg. French vanilla pudding
4 chocolate covered peanut butter cups; chopped
2 c. thawed whipped topping
1 plain Hershey bar; shaved

Combine peanut butter and powdered sugar; blend with fork until smooth. Spread in the bottom of the baked pie crust. Place milk and sour cream in a large bowl; add pudding mix and beat for 2 minutes until thickened. Pour ½ of the filling over the peanut butter mixture Sprinkle the chopped candy bar evenly over the pie. Top with remaining pudding. Spread with whipped topping, and then sprinkle shaved chocolate on top. Chill until firm. Serves 6.

SIMPLE TIRAMISU

3 c. sponge cake, cubed
2 envelopes instant mocha cappuccino
2 c. cold milk, divided
1 (8-oz.) pkg. soft cream cheese
1 sm. pkg. vanilla instant pudding
2 c. thawed whipped topping
1 semi sweet chocolate bar (shaved)

Cover bottom of an 8-inch glass, square pan with cake. Dissolve 1 envelope of cappuccino with 1/2 c. milk. Sprinkle over cake. Beat cream cheese until smooth; gradually add the rest of the milk, pudding mix and 1 envelope of cappuccino; beat at low speed until blended. Stir in whipped topping; spoon over cake evenly and top with shaved chocolate. Refrigerate for at least 3 hours before serving. Serves 6.

MUD PIE

8 oz. Oreo cookie crumbs
1/2 c. melted butter
3 c. chocolate ice cream, softened
3 c. vanilla ice cream, softened
1 can whipped topping
Chocolate fudge

Mix Oreo crumbs and butter together well, pat down in a 10-inch pie plate. Place ice cream in a bowl and blend just enough for a marble effect. Spoon onto crust evenly. Drizzle chocolate fudge over ice cream then place in freezer until fudge has hardened, then cover with waxed paper. Freeze for at least 12 hours before serving. Lay the piece of pie on its side when serving, and squirt the side up with the whipped topping. Serves 6.

MOUSSE TRIFLE

2½ c. cold milk
⅓ c. instant coffee granules
2 sm. pkgs. vanilla instant pudding
2 (8-oz.) containers of thawed whipped topping
1 sponge cake; cut in 1-inch cubes
1 oz. square semi sweet chocolate; grated
¼ tsp. cinnamon

In a bowl whisk milk and coffee, let stand 5 minutes to dissolve. Set aside 1 cup of the milk mixture Add pudding mix to the remaining milk mixture, whisk until it begins to thicken. Fold in 1 container of whipped topping. Using a chilled large glass bowl, place ⅓ of the cake in bottom; pour the 1-cup of reserved milk mixture over the top, evenly. Top with ⅓ of the pudding mixture. Sprinkle ¼ of the grated chocolate on top. Repeat layers 2 more times. Spread remaining container of whipped topping over all. Sprinkle with cinnamon and use the rest of the grated chocolate for the center of the dessert. Serves 6.

SIMPLY SINFUL CHOCOLATE PIE

1 large Hershey's Symphony Bar, plain chocolate
1 (6 oz.) carton chocolate Cool Whip
1 Oreo pie crust
4 oz. regular Cool Whip

Break chocolate bar into pieces, place in a glass bowl reserving 2 squares for topping. Microwave for 30 to 45 seconds, stir. Add chocolate Cool Whip to melted chocolate, blend by stirring. Pour into crust Top with a layer of regular cool whip grate the reserved chocolate on top. Refrigerate at least 2 hours. Serves 4-6.

CHERRY PRETZEL CAKE

2 c. crushed salted pretzels
½ c. butter, melted
½ c. sugar
8 oz. softened cream cheese
⅓ c. powder sugar
2 envelopes Dream Whip
1 lg. can cherry pie filling

Mix the first 3 ingredients and press into an 8 x 8 glass pan. Blend cream cheese and the powdered sugar together. In a separate bowl, prepare dream whip as directed, then combine the cheese and the whipped topping together, beat until smooth. Spread mixture over the pretzel crust and refrigerate over night. The next day spread cherry pie filling on top. Refrigerate until serving. Serves 6-8.

NO ROLL PIE CRUST

1 (9-inch) glass pie plate
1½ c. flour
1 T. sugar
½ tsp. salt
½ c. canola oil
3 T. milk

Preheat oven to 375 degrees. Combine all ingredients in a bowl and mix with fork. Pour into pie plate and push the pastry up the sides to form a nice edge with your thumb and finger. Prick bottom with fork several times. For non-bake pie fillings bake in a 375 degree preheated oven for 15 - 17 minutes or until golden brown. Follow baking instructions for recipes that the filling does need to be baked.

CHOCOLATE CHERRY BANANA CREAM PIE

1 (8 oz.) package cream cheese, softened
½ c. sugar
1 c. mashed ripe banana
1 tsp. lemon juice
1 (8 oz.) carton whipped topping
1 (9 in.) Oreo crust
1 (21 oz.) can cherry pie filling
Canned whipped topping

In a bowl, beat cream cheese and sugar until smooth. Combine bananas and lemon juice; add to cream cheese mixture. Fold in whipped topping. Pour into crust. Cover and refrigerate for 1 hour or until set. Spoon cherry pie filling evenly over pie, slice and serve with a squirt of topping.

CHOCOLATE CARAMEL PECAN PIE

1 c. crushed Oreo cookies
⅓ c. melted butter
24 caramels
½ c. whipping cream, divided

2 c. chopped pecans
1 c. semi sweet chocolate chips
Whipped topping

Combine cookie crumbs and melted butter. Press onto the bottom of a 9-in. pie plate. In a saucepan, melt caramels with ¼ cup cream over low heat; stir until blended. Remove from the heat; stir in pecans. Spread evenly over crust. Refrigerate until set, about 15 minutes. Using another small saucepan melt chocolate chips with remaining cream. Drizzle the chocolate mixture over the caramel layer. Refrigerate at least 1½ hours before serving. Top with whipped topping. Serves 6.

Recipe Favorites

Recipe Favorites

Specialty Drinks

SPECIALTY DRINKS

HOT CHOCOLATE ALMOND

2 oz. butterscotch schnapps
½ oz. amaretto
5 oz. hot chocolate
Whipped topping

Pour into coffee mug and top with whipped cream. Makes 1 serving.

CHOCOLATE COFFEE KISS

¾ oz. coffee liqueur
¾ oz. Irish cream
1 splash brown Crème de Cocoa
1 splash Grand Marnier
1½ oz. chocolate syrup
Hot coffee
1 chocolate bar, shaved
Whipped cream or topping

Pour liqueurs into a mug, fill with hot coffee. Top with whipped cream & shaved chocolate. Makes 1 serving.

RUSSIAN COFFEE

½ oz. coffee liqueur
½ oz. hazelnut liqueur
¼ oz. vodka
Hot coffee
Whipped topping
pinch Cocoa powder, cinnamon & nutmeg

Pour alcohol into a mug, fill with hot coffee. Top with whipped cream; sprinkle with cocoa powder, cinnamon and nutmeg.

THE ORGASM

2 oz. vodka
2 oz. Amaretto
2 oz. Kahlua
2 oz. light cream

Mix ingredients in a shaker of ice, strain and serve in shot glasses or shooter. Makes 4 servings

CHOCOLATE BANANA SMASH

2 oz. Irish Cream
2 oz. Kahlua
1 oz. milk
2 scoop vanilla ice cream
½ med. banana
1 oz. chocolate syrup
½ c. ice
Whipped cream
Chocolate sprinkles

Blend the first 7 ingredients until smooth. Pour into glass and top with whipped cream and chocolate sprinkles. May add a cherry and a small slice of banana on top. Serves 2.

CHI-CHI

1½ oz. vodka
1 oz. cream of coconut
4 oz. pineapple juice
1 c. ice

Blend ingredients until smooth. Serves 2.

TIDAL WAVE

1¼ oz. melon liqueur
1 oz. pineapple Juice
1 oz. orange juice
½ oz. coconut syrup
1½ oz. sour mix
½ oz. rum
1 c. ice
Lime slices
Cherries

Blend until smooth. Pour into small glass. Put a lime slice on the edge of the glass, add a cherry. Serves 2.

SONIC BLASTER

1 oz. vodka
1 oz. light rum
1 oz. banana liqueur
2 oz. pineapple juice
2 oz. orange juice
2 oz. cranberry juice
Ice
Orange or lime slices

Shake all ingredients and pour into a martini glass with ice, garnish with an orange and lime slice. Serves 2.

BOSTON GOLD PUNCH

8 oz. vodka
4 oz. cream de banana
32 oz. orange juice Ice

Mix together and pour over ice, or serve in punch bowl. Makes 8 servings.

WOO-HOO

3 oz. vodka
2 oz. peach schnapps
2 oz. cranberry juice

Mix with ice in a shaker, strain into a highball glass and serve. Serves 2.

HOME MADE IRISH CREAM

2 eggs
2 T. chocolate syrup
1½ tsp. vanilla
9 oz. inexpensive brandy
1 can Eagle Brand sweetened condensed milk
½ pt. whipping cream

In blender add eggs, blend until foamy. Add next chocolate syrup, vanilla and brandy, blend again. Last add sweetened milk and whipping cream. Blend well, store in refrigerator for up to one month. Shake before serving. Makes one-fifth for ⅓ of the cost.

KAHLUA

2 qts. water
⅝ c. instant coffee
6 c. sugar
2 oz. pure vanilla extract
½ gal. vodka

Bring to boil 1 qt. water and the coffee. Cool. In a separate saucepan add the other qt. of water and the sugar. Bring to boil, stirring and cook until sugar is dissolved, cool. Add the two above mixtures together and add the vanilla extract, stir. Now add the vodka, stir well, pour into bottles, cap and store for 4 weeks before serving. Makes 1 gallon.

THE HEALTHY MARTINI

1½ c. pomegranate juice
6 oz. orange vodka

4 ice cubes
Orange slices, cut in quarters

In a shaker place juice, vodka and ice cubes. Shake to mix and chill, strain in a martini glass. Garnish with an orange slice. Serves 1

Recipe Favorites

Family Favorites

FAMILY FAVORITES

CRAB BREAKFAST SCRAMBLE

2 T. melted butter or margarine
12 eggs
½ c. milk
1 tsp. garlic salt
½ tsp. pepper, white or black
1½ tsp. chopped fresh dill weed, or ½ tsp. dried
1 c. chopped crab meat, may use canned but drain well
1 (8-oz.) pkg. cream cheese, cut in cubes
2 med. green onions, sliced
Sprinkles of paprika

Pour butter into 8 x 8 x 2 baking dish, tilt pan to coat bottom. Beat eggs, milk, salt, pepper, and dill in lg. bowl using whisk or fork. Stir in crabmeat, cream cheese and onions. Pour into baking dish. Cover and refrigerate up to 24 hours. Pre-heat oven to 350°, sprinkle paprika on top before baking. Bake uncovered 45 to 50 min, or until center is set. Serves 4 to 6.

MEXICAN BREAKFAST

1-2 lbs. ground sausage
½ lb. sliced mushrooms
1 med. onion chipped
12 lg. eggs
3 T. sour cream
6 T. your favorite salsa
8 oz. shredded mozzarella cheese
8 oz. shredded cheddar cheese
Salt & pepper to taste

Preheat oven to 400°. Brown sausage, mushrooms, onions, and drain. Combine eggs, sour cream, whip together, and pour in 9x13 baking pan. Bake 10 min. and remove from oven. Turn oven down to 325°. Spoon salsa over eggs, then sausage, and top with cheeses. Bake for 30 minutes, or until cheese is melted. Serves 8 to 10.

24 HOUR BREAKFAST CASSEROLE

- 1 lb. pork sausage
- 2 ½ c. seasoned croutons
- 10 eggs
- 2 ¼ c. milk
- 1 can (10.75 oz.) cream of mushroom soup
- 1 (10 oz.) pkg. frozen chopped spinach, thawed and squeezed dry.
- ½ c. chopped onion
- 1 (4.5 oz.) can mushrooms, drained and chopped
- 1 c. sharp shredded cheddar cheese
- 1 c. shredded Monterey Jack cheese
- ¼ tsp. dried mustard
- Fresh parsley for garnish

Spread croutons on the bottom of a 9 X 13 baking dish. Crumble sausage into skillet, cook over medium heat until browned. Drain and spread over croutons. In a large bowl whisk together eggs and milk until well blended. Stir in soup, spinach, onions, mushrooms, cheeses and mustard. Pour egg mixture evenly over sausage and croutons. Refrigerate overnight. In the morning, preheat oven to 325°. Bake for 50 to 55 minutes or until lightly brown. Let stand 10 minutes to set. Serve with parsley garnish. Serves 8.

QUICHE CASSEROLE

- 4-5 c. Italian bread, cubed, no crust
- 2 c. diced ham, cooked sausage or cooked bacon
- 1 c. canned mushrooms, drained well
- ¾ c. chopped onion
- ¾ c. chopped green pepper
- 2 c. shredded cheddar cheese
- 1 c. shredded Swiss cheese
- 10 eggs
- 3 c. milk
- Salt and pepper to taste.

Prepare 24 hours in advance. Using a 9x13-baking dish, layer the first 7 ingredients in order given. Blend together eggs, milk, salt and pepper. Pour evenly over the cheese layer. Cover and refrigerate for about 24 hours. Bake covered in a pre-heated 350° oven for 30 minutes, remove cover and bake 30 more minutes. Cover loosely and let stand 10 minutes until set. Serves 6 to 8. May substitute or omit a vegetable and also use egg beaters instead of eggs.

BENEDICT BRUNCH EGGS

10-12 slices Canadian bacon or ham slices
12 oz. shredded Swiss cheese
12 lg. eggs
1 c. whipping cream
½ tsp. garlic salt
½ tsp. pepper
¼ tsp. basil
½ c. grated Parmesan cheese
1 tsp. paprika

Cut bacon or ham into small pieces. Place in a lightly greased 9x13 baking dish to cover the bottom. Sprinkle with Swiss cheese. Break eggs over the cheese, spacing evenly. Do not break yolks. Pour whipping cream over eggs, sprinkle with salt, pepper, and basil. Bake at 425° for 15 min. Remove from oven; sprinkle the Parmesan cheese and paprika. Bake another 8 to 10 minutes or when set. Let stand 10 minutes before serving. Serve on the side, or on top of a toasted English muffin. Serves 8.

DAUGHTERS FAVORITE CHICKEN CASSEROLE

4 c. cook and cubed chicken
1 c. chopped celery
⅓ c. chopped onion
1 c. mayonnaise
1 ½ tsp. lemon juice
Pepper to taste
2 c. shredded taco cheese
¾ c. crushed potato chips

Mix everything together except the potato chips, then spoon into an ungreased, 2 quart baking dish. Top with ¾ cup crushed potato chips. Bake for 1 hour at 350 degrees. Serves 4.

CHICKEN POT PIE

2 Pillsbury pie crusts
Non stick cooking spray
2 c. cooked cubed chicken breasts
1 can cream of chicken soup
½ can milk
1 c. frozen chunk potatoes, thawed
1 can corn, drained
¼ c. chopped onion
½ c. canned and drained mushrooms
½ c. canned or frozen sliced carrots, thawed
¼ tsp. garlic salt
Pepper to taste

Coat a 9 inch pie dish with cooking spray, place 1 crust in bottom of the dish. Save the other one for the top. In a 2 quart saucepan combine the rest of the ingredients. Stir well and heat to a boil over medium heat. Pour into pie plate, top with the other crust, seal, and flute edges of crust. Cut 3 scallops out of top pie crust, or prick with fork 4 to 5 times for venting. Bake as directed on crust package. Serve hot. Makes 4 - 5 servings.

CHICKEN OR TURKEY TETRAZZINI

½ c. butter
2 cans cream of mushroom soup
¼ tsp. garlic salt
⅛ tsp. white pepper
½ c. chicken broth
2 cups cooked chicken or turkey, cubed fine (leftovers are great)
½ lb. spaghetti, cooked and drained
½ c. diced celery
½ c. chopped onion
3 (oz.) Parmesan cheese

In a large saucepan melt butter; add soup, spices and chicken broth. Heat over medium until warmed. Add everything else except the Parmesan cheese and stir well. Spoon into glass casserole dish and sprinkle Parmesan cheese evenly on top. Bake covered, at 350 degrees for 30 to 40 minutes. Serves 6.

CHICKEN QUESADILLAS

2 c. cooked shredded chicken
1¼ c. Monterey Jack cheese, shredded
½ c. thinly sliced red onion
⅛ c. mayonnaise
2 T. chopped sun dried tomatoes in oil

2 T. water
¼ tsp. pepper
8 flour tortillas
4 tsp. olive oil

Heat oven to 425 degrees. lightly spray a large cookie sheet with oil. Combine all ingredients except the tortillas and the oil. Spread ½ cup chicken mixture on 4 of the tortilla's. Top each with another tortilla shell. Brush tops with olive oil, covering well. Bake 10 - 12 minutes until lightly brown. Cut into pie wedges. Serve on the side with your choice of the following: sour cream, salsa, and or guacamole. Ranch dressing is also excellent. Makes 4 pies. You may substitute the tomatoes for chili peppers or anything of your choice.

CHICKEN ENCHILADAS

1 (9 oz.) bag spinach
1 (11-oz.) can cream of chicken soup
½ c. sour cream
1 T. butter
½ onion, chopped
¾ tsp. chili powder

2 c. shredded cooked chicken breast
½ c. sweet banana peppers, chopped
1½ c. shredded cheddar cheese
6 (8 in.) flour tortillas

Preheat oven to 350 degrees. Sauté spinach in fry pan with a buttery spray oil, just until soft. In a small bowl mix soup and sour cream; set aside. Melt butter in a med. saucepan over med. high heat. Add onion and chili powder, sauté until tender. Stir in chicken, peppers and 2 T. of soup mixture. Stir and cook until heated. Remove from heat and stir in spinach and ½ c. cheese. Spread about ¾ cup of the soup mixture down the center of each tortilla, roll up and place seam side down in baking dish. Spoon remaining soup on top and sprinkle with 1 cup of cheese. Bake for 25 minutes, or until bubbly. Serves 4.

SANDIE'S MANICOTTI

- 8 oz. lasagna noodles
- 1 (48-oz.) jar Prego spaghetti sauce, any flavor
- 1 tsp. dried basil
- 1/8 c. sugar
- 1/4 tsp. garlic salt
- 1 lb. ricotta cheese
- 3 c. shredded mozzarella, reserve half for topping
- 1/2 c. Parmesan cheese, grated, reserve 1/4 c. for topping
- 1 egg, slightly beaten with fork
- 1/3 c. Italian bread crumbs
- 1/4 c. fresh chopped parsley

Preheat oven to 375 degrees. Prepare noodles as directed, cooking 3 minutes less than what is called for. Drain, rinse, and dry out on paper towel. Cut in half to make 2 four inch or so pieces of each. In a medium size bowl combine sauce, basil, sugar, and garlic salt. Stir together and set aside. In a separate smaller bowl combine ricotta, 1/2 of the mozzarella, 1/2 of the Parmesan, beaten egg, bread crumbs, and parsley. Mix together well. Spoon 1/2 of the sauce mixture on the bottom of 9x13 baking pan. Spoon onto one end of noodle 1 heaping tablespoon of cheese mixture. Roll up, starting at cheese end and place on sauce in pan, seam side down. Repeat until you are out of cheese mixture. Pour remaining sauce evenly over the manicottis. Top with remaining 1/4 c. Parmesan and the remaining mozzarella. Cover with foil and bake for 15 minutes. Remove foil and bake for another 15 minutes. May make ahead and store in refrigerator but add 5 minutes more to baking time. Makes 16 and serves 8.

MY MOM'S MEAT LOAF

- 2 lbs. ground beef
- 1 c. quick oats
- 2 eggs, slightly beaten
- 1 T. Worcestershire
- 1/2 c. chopped onion
- 1 tsp. salt
- 1/2 tsp. garlic salt
- 1/2 tsp. pepper
- 3/4 c. ketchup mixed with 1 T. brown sugar

Pre-heat oven to 350 degrees. In large bowl combine all ingredients except ketchup and brown sugar. Mix well. Pack well in a loaf pan. Combine ketchup and brown sugar, spread on top of meat loaf. Bake for 45 minutes, remove from oven and let stand 5 minutes before slicing. Serves 4-6.

CABBAGE PIGGY ROLLS

1 head cabbage, rinsed
1 onion, chopped
2 tsp. minced garlic
3 T. butter
1 c. cooked wild rice or white rice
1 lb. ground round
1 lb. Italian pork sausage
1 tsp. seasoned pepper
2 tsp. dried dill weed
1 tsp. basil
2 tsp. Montreal steak seasoning

Sauce:
2 (11-oz.) cans tomato bisque soup
1 can stew tomatoes, drained
1 can diced tomatoes with mild chilies, drained
¼ tsp. tarragon
2 tsp. sugar
½ tsp. seasoned pepper
½ tsp. garlic salt
6 Bay leaves, reserve for top

Freeze cabbage head the night before. Remove from freezer and let stand to thaw. Leaves will peel right off. Sauté onions and garlic in the butter and add to the rest of the ingredients except the sauce. Mix well. Make mini loafs with 2 to 3 tablespoons of the meat mixture. Place on a cabbage leave. Bring one end of cabbage leaf over loaf, roll once then tuck ends inside to prevent filling from falling out. Place in an oil sprayed 9 x 13 glass-baking dish. With a blender add all ingredients for the sauce. Blend until mixed. Do not purée. Pour over cabbage rolls, top with bay leaves. Cover with aluminum foil. Bake for 2 to 2½ hours depending upon size, in a 350° preheated oven. Let cool 15 minutes before removing foil. Serves 6.

BACON WRAPPED PORK LOIN ROAST

3 cloves of garlic
2 lbs. boneless pork loin

6 strips uncooked bacon
Salt & pepper

Preheat oven to 325°. Peel garlic and cut each clove in half. Using the tip of knife make holes in the top of the loin about an inch apart. Place the garlic pieces inside of the holes. Sprinkle salt and pepper all over it, then wrap with bacon slices. Place in glass baking dish, cover with foil and bake for 1 ½ hours or until done to your likeness. Remove from oven, unwrap the bacon and discard. Slice and serve.

NO PEEK SWISS STEAK

1 T. butter, melted
2 lbs. round steak;, cut in serving size pieces
1 (14 oz.) stewed tomatoes, reserve 1/2 c. juice
1 envelope onion soup mix, sprinkled evenly
1 (13 oz.) can mushrooms, drained
1 T. A-1 steak sauce
1 T. cornstarch or Wondra
1 T. fresh parsley

Preheat oven to 375°. Place foil in a 9x13 pan. Pour and spread melted butter on the foil. Place steak pieces in pan. Layer in order, tomatoes, onion soup mix, and mushrooms. Mix together steak sauce, reserved tomato juice and Wondra/cornstarch. Pour over mushrooms evenly. Cover with foil and bake for 2 1/2 hours. Don't peek now. Remove from oven and sprinkle with fresh, chopped parsley. Serves 4-6.

SEAFOOD LINGUINE CASSEROLE

12 oz. linguine, cooked as directed, drain
2 14 oz. can diced tomatoes with chilies
1/2 c. white wine
1/2 c. bloody mary mix
2 T. olive oil
1 T. minced garlic
1 tsp. salt
1/2 tsp. dried basil
1/4 tsp. pepper blend
1 T. parsley
2 T. sugar
1 T. Wondra
6 oz. cooked shrimp, fresh or frozen, shelled and de-tailed
6 oz. fresh or frozen sea scallops, halved if large
1/2 c. Parmesan cheese
2 c. shredded cheddar or Colby cheese

While preparing linguine, bring to boil over med. heat the next 10 ingredients. Stir in wondra, reduce to simmer and cook uncovered for 20 minutes. Add frozen shrimp and scallops or any seafood of your choice. Cook for 5 to 10 minutes longer until scallops are opaque and shrimp is done. Place hot linguine in a lightly oil sprayed glass baking dish, sprinkle with Parmesan cheese. Then spoon the hot linguine over the noodles evenly. Top with grated shredded cheese. Broil until cheese is melted. Serves 6.

COD AND SHRIMP CASSEROLE

1 can cream of shrimp soup
6 cod filets
½ tsp. dill weed
2 c. shredded Colby cheese
½ lb. cooked shrimp, shelled and untailed
1 c. crushed buttery crackers
½ c. milk

Preheat oven to 400°. In a 8 x 8 baking dish spread ¼ of the soup on the bottom. Layer in order, cod, dill, 1 cup of cheese, shrimp, the rest of soup, cracker crumbs, last cup of cheese and then milk. Bake uncovered for 40 minutes. Serves 4.

SPAGHETTI PIE

6 (oz.) spaghetti, cook as directed
2 T. butter
⅓ c. grated Parmesan cheese
2 eggs, well beaten
1 c. cottage cheese
1 lb. ground beef
½ c. onion, chopped
¼ c. green pepper, chopped
1 (8-oz.) can tomatoes, cut up or blended
1 (6-oz.) can tomato paste
2 tsp. sugar
1 tsp. oregano
½ tsp. garlic salt
¾ c. mozzarella cheese

Drain noodles and stir in butter while they are hot. Add Parmesan cheese and eggs, stir again. In a 10 inch pie plate, add spaghetti and form into a crust. Spread cottage cheese on the bottom of the crust layer. In skillet cook beef, onion and green pepper until meat is browned. Drain and stir in tomatoes, paste, sugar, oregano and garlic salt: heat through. Spread meat mixture into pie. Bake uncovered at 350° for 20 minutes. Sprinkle mozzarella cheese on top and bake 5 minutes longer or until cheese melts. Serves 6.

BAKED PASTA ITALIANO

1 lb. ground beef
1/4 c. chopped onion
1/4 c. green pepper, chopped
1 clove minced garlic
1 (6-oz.) can tomato paste
1/3 c. water
1 tsp. garlic salt
1 T. sugar
1/2 tsp. oregano leaves
2 c. spaghetti noodles, cooked and drained
1/4 c. chopped parsley
1/2 c. Miracle Whip
3/4 c. grated Parmesan cheese
2 eggs, beaten

Brown meat, drain. Add onion, green pepper and garlic, cook until tender. Add tomato paste, water and all seasonings; stir together. Combine noodles and parsley; toss lightly. In a separate bowl combine Miracle Whip, 1/2 cup of the Parmesan cheese and eggs; mix well. Layer noodles, salad dressing mixture, and meat sauce in a 10 x 6 baking dish. Top with remaining cheese. Bake at 350 degrees for 25 minutes. Serves 4-6.

ITALIAN RIGATONI

1 box rigatoni pasta
1 c. slivered almonds
1 pkg. garlic & herb croutons
2 T. butter
1 (7 oz.) jar sundried tomatoes in oil

Cook pasta as directed in boiling salted water. While that is cooking sauté almonds in a hot small fry pan, tossing until lightly browned. Combine croutons and almonds, blend or chop. Drain water from pasta, place pasta back into pot. Add butter, stir until butter is melted, then add crouton mixture, toss lightly. Stir in sun dried tomatoes and oil, serve in a pasta bowl. You may use a jar of roasted red peppers instead of tomatoes. Serves 4-6.

RED SKIN POTATOES WITH LEEKS

12 sm. redskin potatoes, washed
3 leeks, washed well and dried.
3 sprigs of fresh rosemary
¾ stick of real butter, melted
1 T. minced garlic
½ tsp. garlic salt
Pepper to taste

Wash potatoes, poke with fork and microwave 6 at a time for about 4 minutes. This will cut down on cooking time. Cool, cut each potato into 4's and place in gallon size freezer bag. Slice only the whites of the leeks, discard the greens and add them to the bag of potatoes. Cut off and use only the leaves of the rosemary, add to potatoes along with the rest of the ingredients. Seal up bag, shake well to mix. Pour into a foil pan, grill on med. high heat, stirring once, until lightly browned, or bake in oven for 20 to 30 minutes at 375°.

SIMPLE ROASTED REDSKIN POTATOES

6 med. red skinned potatoes, cut into eighths
2 T. canola oil
¾ tsp. onion powder
1 tsp. McCormick Garlic Pepper seasoning
¼ tsp. paprika
1 T. fresh chopped dill

Place potatoes in a greased 9x13-inch baking pan. In a small bowl combine oil, onion powder, garlic pepper seasoning, and paprika. Drizzle oil mixture drizzle over potatoes, tossing to coat. Roast, uncovered, in a 325 degrees oven for 45 minutes. Remove from oven, stir in chives and bake for 10 to 20 minutes more or until potatoes are tender and brown on the edges. Serves 6-8.

EASY BAKED BEAN CASSEROLE

1 lg. jar Northern beans, drained
½ c. brown sugar
½ med. onion, chopped
½ lb. bacon, cooked and drained
1 T. prepared mustard
⅓ c. ketchup
Tomato juice

In a large bowl add all ingredients except tomato juice and mix well; then add enough tomato juice to make it soupy, stir. Place in a 2-quart baking dish, bake at 375 degrees for 45 minutes or until thickened and done. Stir occasionally. Serves 6.

ZUCCHINI CASSEROLE

3 Zucchini, sliced ¼ inch thick
½ c. sliced onions
2 c. mushrooms, quartered
1 T. minced garlic

1 can Italian diced or stewed tomatoes, drained
1 T. Worcestershire sauce
½ c. Parmesan cheese

In an oiled sprayed fry pan, sauté zucchini, onions, mushrooms and garlic for 5 minutes. Drain, then place in 2 quart casserole dish. Stir in tomatoes and worcestershire sauce. Top with cheese. Bake in a 350° oven for 30 minutes. Serves 4.

BANANA SPLIT PIE

1 stick of butter, softened
1 c. flour
2 T. water
3 T. crushed pecans
1 (8 oz.) pkg. cream cheese
1 c. powdered sugar
1-2 bananas, sliced

1 (3 oz.) pkg. instant banana cream pie filling, prepare as directed
(8-oz.) whipped topping, spread evenly
½ c. Hershey's chocolate syrup
½ c. chopped pecans

Blend butter, flour, water and crushed pecans with fork, press into 9-inch pie plate. Prick with fork several times. Bake in a 400° oven for 12 to 15 minutes. Do not burn! Cool. Blend together cream cheese and powdered sugar. Spread on to cooled crust evenly. Place bananas in single layer on top of cooled crust. Spread pudding over bananas, then whipped topping. Drizzle with chocolate syrup and top with pecans. Refrigerate for at least 2 hours before serving. Serves 6.

AWARD WINNING CHOCOLATE LOVER BROWNIE SQUARES

1 box chunk chocolate brownie mix
1 pkg. (10 ounces) sweet flaked coconut
1 pkg. (11.5 ounces) semi sweet chocolate chunks
1 can (14 ounces) sweetened condensed milk
1 pkg. (2.25 ounces) sliced almonds

Preheat oven to 350°. Spray 9x13 pan with nonstick cooking spray. Prepare brownie mix as directed on pkg. for cake-like brownies. Spread evenly in pan. Bake 20 minutes, or until brownies are set.....Do not over bake! Remove from oven. Layer coconut and chocolate chunks on top of brownies. Pour sweetened condensed milk evenly over coconut and chocolate chunks, sprinkle with almonds. Return brownies to oven and bake for 25 minutes, or until coconut is golden brown and almonds are toasty. Run a sharp knife along the edges while hot. This will prevent sticking. Cool completely on a rack, cut into small bars when cool. Serves 8.

OVEN CARAMEL CORN

12 c. popped popcorn
¾ c. salted almonds
¾ c. cashews
1 c. packed brown sugar
½ c. butter
¼ c. light corn syrup
¼ tsp. salt
½ tsp. baking soda

Heat oven to 200°. Divide popcorn and nuts between 2 ungreased roasting pans or 9 x 13 rectangular pans. Heat brown sugar, butter, corn syrup and salt in saucepan over medium heat. Cook while stirring until bubbly, 5 - 10 minutes. Remove from heat. Stir in baking soda. Pour mixture over popcorn and nuts, stir until well coated. Bake 1 hour, stirring every 15 minutes.

POTATO CHIP COOKIES

1 c. brown sugar
1 c. white sugar
1 c. margarine
2 eggs
1 ½ c. flour

2 c. oatmeal
2 c. crushed potato chips
1 tsp. baking powder
1 tsp. vanilla

Preheat oven to 350°. In a lg. bowl combine sugars, margarine and eggs, beat until creamy. Add the rest of the ingredients, blend well together. Drop by tablespoon on to ungreased cookie sheet. Bake for 10 to 12 minutes until a light golden brown. Cookies should be chewy, not hard. Makes 2 dozen.

OATMEAL CAKE

1 ½ c. water
1 c. quick oats
½ c. margarine
2 eggs
1 c. sugar
1 c. brown sugar
1 ½ c. flour
½ tsp. cinnamon

1 tsp. baking soda
½ tsp. salt
Topping:
1 T. soft butter
½ c. brown sugar
¼ c. milk
½ c. chopped pecans
½ c. coconut

Bring water to boil in small saucepan. Add oats, stir until no lumps. Let cool in refrigerator. Combine margarine, eggs, and sugars. Beat well with mixer then add; flour, cinnamon, soda and salt. Mix well. Pour into a 9x13 lightly greased baking pan. Bake for 45 to 50 minutes at 350°. While cake is baking, prepare topping in a small bowl. Mix together by hand soft butter, brown sugar, milk, pecans, and coconut. Spread on top of hot cake, let cool and serve.

DAD'S FAVORITE BANANA CAKE

3-4 sliced bananas, ripe but NOT brown
2 c. sugar
2 eggs
2/3 c. vegetable oil
1 c. sour milk; add 1 T. of vinegar or lemon juice to milk for souring
2 1/2 c. flour
1 tsp. baking powder
1 tsp. baking soda
1 tsp. vanilla
Pinch of salt

Preheat oven to 375°. Beat together bananas, sugar, eggs, then add the rest of the ingredients and mix together well. Pour into a greased and floured 9x13 cake pan, or 2 round cake pans. Bake for 10 minutes at 375°, then turn oven down to 350°, and bake for 30 minutes longer or when toothpick comes out clean from center.

7-UP CHOCOLATE CAKE

1 c. brown sugar
1 c. granulated sugar
1/2 c. margarine
2 eggs
3/4 c. 7-up
2 c. flour
2 tsp. baking soda
3/4 c. cocoa
1 c. boiling water

Mix in order listed. Pour into a greased 9x13 pan. Bake at 350° for 30 to 35 minutes.

WHIP CREAM FROSTING

1/4 c. flour
1 c. milk
1 c. softened butter
1 c. sugar
1 tsp. vanilla, or almond extract

In saucepan, over medium heat, dissolve flour in milk, stirring constantly, no lumps. Bring to boil. It should be thick. Remove from stove, place a sheet of waxed paper on top of mixture to prevent it from getting air and hardening. Refrigerator until cool. In a separate bowl, beat the butter, sugar and extract until creamy and almost white. Add the two mixtures together when flour and milk are cooled. Beat until creamy and sugar granules are dissolved.

UNIQUE CHOCOLATE FROSTING

1 T. butter
2 squares (1 oz. each) unsweetened sweet
1 egg
½ c. whipping cream
1 ½ c. powdered sugar
1 tsp. vanilla

Melt together while stirring butter and chocolate. In a small bowl combine the rest of the ingredients and mix well. Add the 2 mixtures together, beat on med. high until the frosting holds a peak.

Recipe Favorites

INDEX OF RECIPES

BREAKFAST

BACON SWISS QUICHE	2
EASY BREAKFAST BRUNCH	3
EGG MUFFIN SANDWICH	2
OMELETTE FOR ONE	2
POTATO PANCAKE	1
SCRAMBLED EGG BURRITO	1

APPETIZERS & MUNCHIES

BACON WRAPPED SHRIMP OR SCALLOPS	5
BEEF ROLL-UPS	7
BLT DIP	6
BOATERS CUCUMBER DILL DIP	9
CHOCOLATE MALT SNACK MIX	12
CHOCOLATE NUT CLUSTERS	10
CRAB FONDUE	6
CREAMY DILLED SHRIMP	9
DILLY DIP FOR VEGETABLES	9
GRANOLA FRUIT SNACK	11
GUACAMOLE & CREAM CHEESE DIP	8
JUMBO SHRIMP WITH HOME MADE COCKTAIL SAUCE	7
MICROWAVE PEANUT BRITTLE (SO EASY!!!)	10
NUTS AND BOLTS	11
OYSTER CRACKER SNACK	10
PROSCIUTTO AND MELON CANAPAS	8
PUPPY CHOW	12
SALMON DILL MINI SANDWICHES	8
VEGGIE SNACK SAUCE	7
YUMMY PIZZA DIP	5

SOUPS & SANDWICHES

CHICKEN CAESAR WRAP	21
CHICKEN GUMBO SOUP	17
CHICKEN NOODLE SOUP	16
CHICKEN OR TURKEY ALFREDO SOUP	19
CLASSIC FRIED EGG SANDWICH	22
CREAM OF BROCCOLI SOUP	13
CREAM OF TOMATO SOUP	14
FRENCH ONION SOUP	14
GERMAN HAM SANDWICH	22
GOURMET GRILLED CHEESE	20
MY EASY HAM AND BEAN SOUP	19
MY SPECIAL ITALIAN SAUSAGE SOUP	17
ORIENTAL SHRIMP SOUP	20
ROAST BEEF WRAPS WITH CHEESE SAUCE	21
SANDIE'S AWARD WINNING LOUISIANA STYLE CHILI	16
SANDIE'S BAKED POTATO SOUP	13
SANDIE'S UNIQUE TACO SOUP	18
SEAFOOD SALAD SANDWICH	21
SIMPLE MINESTRONE SOUP	15
SMOKED SEAFOOD GUMBO	18
TUNA SALAD ON RAISIN BREAD	20
TURKEY CROISSANT WITH CRANBERRIES	22
VEGETABLE BEEF & BARLEY SOUP	15
YUMMY CHEESE AND BLACK BEAN SOUP	15

SALADS & VEGETABLES

BROCCOLI AND EGG SALAD	24
CHERRY BROCCOLI SALAD	24
DRIED CHERRY CHICKEN SALAD	28
GRILLED CABBAGE	29
GRILLED CHICKEN SESAME SALAD	26
GRILLED CORN ON THE COB WITH HERB BUTTER	30
GRILLED FRESH GREEN BEANS AND BACON	30
GRILLED MIXED VEGETABLES	29
GRILLED ONION BLOSSOM WITH SAUCE	31
GRILLED PARMESAN POTATOES	32
GRILLED, TWICE BAKED POTATOES	32
ITALIAN MOZZARELLA PASTA SALAD	25
LAYERED CAULIFLOWER SALAD	25
LAYERED FRUIT & CHEESE SALAD	27
MANDARIN ORANGE SALAD WITH ALMONDS	28
MICROWAVE SECRET VEGETABLES	31
MOM'S WILTED SPINACH SALAD	23
9 LAYERED SALAD	23

OLD FASHION GERMAN POTATO SALAD	33
PEAS AND PEANUTS	27
ROASTED CHICKEN AND PEAR SALAD	27
SANDIE'S BOWTIE CHICKEN PASTA SALAD	24
SESAME ORANGE ROMAINE SALAD	26
SMOKEY CHEDDAR POTATOES	33
ZUCCHINI GRILL	30

POULTRY, BEEF & PORK

APPLE SAUCE GRILLED CHICKEN	36
BBQ SLOPPY JOES	38
BREAST OF CHICKEN WITH GREEN ONION SAUCE	35
CORNED BEEF BRISKET DINNER/ WITH SAUCE	39
GARLIC CHICKEN	35
GRILLED BEEF FAJITAS	38
GRILLED ITALIAN SAUSAGE	41
GRILLED PESTO STEAK WITH BLEU CHEESE SAUCE	42
GRILLED PORK CHOPS WITH PESTO	40
GRILLED PORK TENDERLOIN WITH MANGO SALSA	40
MARINATED STEAK	39
ORANGE GINGER CHICKEN	37
SESAME GRILLED CHICKEN	36
SIMPLY YUMMY TERIYAKI CHICKEN	36
SNAPPY BBQ PORK CHOPS	41
SOUR CREAM BURGERS	37
THE SPECIAL GRILLED BURGER	37
ZESTY GRILLED PORK CHOPS	41

FISH & SEAFOOD

BLACKENED GROUPER, WHITEFISH, OR COD	44
EASY SHRIMP SCAMPI	46
GRILLED WHISKEY TUNA STEAKS	43
HONEY MUSTARD SALMON	43
HUBBY'S SUPER FRIED WALLEYE OR PERCH	45
LEMON BUTTER FOR FISH	45
SALMON FILETS WITH HOME MADE LEMON BUTTER	44
SAUTÉED SHRIMP WITH VEGETABLES	45

| SHRIMP AND SCALLOP SKEWERS WITH DIPPING SAUCE | 46 |

SAUCES, MARINADES & DRESSINGS

BBQ WHISKEY SAUCE	50
CUCUMBER DILL SAUCE	48
DILL HOLLANDAISE SAUCE FOR GRILLED SALMON	47
MARINATE FOR GRILLED FISH	50
MUSHROOM SAUCE	48
NEW TWIST TARTER SAUCE	48
PORK LOIN GLAZE	50
SALMON GLAZE	49
SALMON GLAZE II	49
SANDIE'S RED WINE VINEGAR SALAD DRESSING	47
SWEET AND SOUR SAUCE FOR CHICKEN OR MEATBALLS	49
TARTAR SAUCE	47

DESSERTS

CHERRY PRETZEL CAKE	56
CHOCOLATE CARAMEL PECAN PIE	57
CHOCOLATE CHERRY BANANA CREAM PIE	56
CHOCOLATE DIPPED FRUIT	52
CHOCOLATE OAT BARS	53
ELEGANT CHERRY OR BLUEBERRY TORTE	52
HEAVENLY PUDDING CAKE	52
MOUSSE TRIFLE	55
MUD PIE	54
NO ROLL PIE CRUST	55
PEANUT BUTTER CANDY BARS	51
PEANUT BUTTER CREAM PIE	53
POPCORN BARS	51
SIMPLE TIRAMISU	54
SIMPLY SINFUL CHOCOLATE PIE	55

SPECIALTY DRINKS

BOSTON GOLD PUNCH	61
CHI-CHI	60
CHOCOLATE BANANA SMASH	60
CHOCOLATE COFFEE KISS	59
HOME MADE IRISH CREAM	61
HOT CHOCOLATE ALMOND	59
KAHLUA	61
RUSSIAN COFFEE	59

SONIC BLASTER	60
THE HEALTHY MARTINI	62
THE ORGASM	59
TIDAL WAVE	60
WOO-HOO	61

FAMILY FAVORITES

AWARD WINNING CHOCOLATE LOVER BROWNIE SQUARES	75
BACON WRAPPED PORK LOIN ROAST	69
BAKED PASTA ITALIANO	72
BANANA SPLIT PIE	74
BENEDICT BRUNCH EGGS	65
CABBAGE PIGGY ROLLS	69
CHICKEN ENCHILADAS	67
CHICKEN OR TURKEY TETRAZZINI	66
CHICKEN POT PIE	66
CHICKEN QUESADILLAS	67
COD AND SHRIMP CASSEROLE	71
CRAB BREAKFAST SCRAMBLE	63
DAD'S FAVORITE BANANA CAKE	77
DAUGHTERS FAVORITE CHICKEN CASSEROLE	65
EASY BAKED BEAN CASSEROLE	73
ITALIAN RIGATONI	72
MEXICAN BREAKFAST	63
MY MOM'S MEAT LOAF	68
NO PEEK SWISS STEAK	70
OATMEAL CAKE	76
OVEN CARAMEL CORN	75
POTATO CHIP COOKIES	76
QUICHE CASSEROLE	64
RED SKIN POTATOES WITH LEEKS	73
SANDIE'S MANICOTTI	68
SEAFOOD LINGUINE CASSEROLE	70
7-UP CHOCOLATE CAKE	77
SIMPLE ROASTED REDSKIN POTATOES	73
SPAGHETTI PIE	71
24 HOUR BREAKFAST CASSEROLE	64
UNIQUE CHOCOLATE FROSTING	78
WHIP CREAM FROSTING	77
ZUCCHINI CASSEROLE	74

78776A-07 4

How to Order

Get additional copies of this cookbook by returning an order form and your check or money order to:

Sandie's Galley
P.O. Box 515
Elk Rapids, MI 49629
www.sandiesgalley.com

SEE WEBSITE FOR QUANTITY DISCOUNTS

Please send me _____ copies of **Recipes From Sandie's Galley** at **$15.00** per copy and **$2.00** for shipping and handling per book. Enclosed is my check or money order for $_____.

Mail Books To:

Name_____

Address_____

City _____ State _____ Zip _____

✂--

Please send me _____ copies of **Recipes From Sandie's Galley** at **$15.00** per copy and **$2.00** for shipping and handling per book. Enclosed is my check or money order for $_____.

Mail Books To:

Name_____

Address_____

City _____ State _____ Zip _____

PANTRY BASICS

A WELL-STOCKED PANTRY provides all the makings for a good meal. With the right ingredients, you can quickly create a variety of satisfying, delicious meals for family or guests. Keeping these items in stock also means avoiding extra trips to the grocery store, saving you time and money. Although everyone's pantry is different, there are basic items you should always have. Add other items according to your family's needs. For example, while some families consider chips, cereals and snacks as must-haves, others can't be without feta cheese and imported olives. Use these basic pantry suggestions as a handy reference list when creating your grocery list. Don't forget refrigerated items like milk, eggs, cheese and butter.

STAPLES

Baker's chocolate
Baking powder
Baking soda
Barbeque sauce
Bread crumbs (plain or seasoned)
Chocolate chips
Cocoa powder
Cornmeal
Cornstarch
Crackers
Flour
Honey
Ketchup
Lemon juice
Mayonnaise or salad dressing
Non-stick cooking spray
Nuts (almonds, pecans, walnuts)
Oatmeal
Oil (olive, vegetable)
Pancake baking mix
Pancake syrup
Peanut butter
Shortening
Sugar (granulated, brown, powdered)
Vinegar

PACKAGED/CANNED FOODS

Beans (canned, dry)
Broth (beef, chicken)
Cake mixes with frosting
Canned diced tomatoes
Canned fruit
Canned mushrooms
Canned soup
Canned tomato paste & sauce
Canned tuna & chicken
Cereal
Dried soup mix
Gelatin (flavored or plain)
Gravies
Jarred Salsa
Milk (evaporated, sweetened condensed)
Non-fat dry milk
Pastas
Rice (brown, white)
Spaghetti sauce

SPICES/SEASONINGS

Basil
Bay leaves
Black pepper
Bouillon cubes (beef, chicken)
Chives
Chili powder
Cinnamon
Mustard (dried, prepared)
Garlic powder or salt
Ginger
Nutmeg
Onion powder or salt
Oregano
Paprika
Parsley
Rosemary
Sage
Salt
Soy sauce
Tarragon
Thyme
Vanilla
Worcestershire sauce
Yeast

Copyright © 2006
Morris Press Cookbooks
All Rights Reserved.

HERBS & SPICES

DRIED VS. FRESH. While dried herbs are convenient, they don't generally have the same purity of flavor as fresh herbs. Ensure dried herbs are still fresh by checking if they are green and not faded. Crush a few leaves to see if the aroma is still strong. Always store them in an air-tight container away from light and heat.

BASIL	Sweet, warm flavor with an aromatic odor. Use whole or ground. Good with lamb, fish, roast, stews, beef, vegetables, dressing and omelets.
BAY LEAVES	Pungent flavor. Use whole leaf but remove before serving. Good in vegetable dishes, seafood, stews and pickles.
CARAWAY	Spicy taste and aromatic smell. Use in cakes, breads, soups, cheese and sauerkraut.
CELERY SEED	Strong taste which resembles the vegetable. Can be used sparingly in pickles and chutney, meat and fish dishes, salads, bread, marinades, dressings and dips.
CHIVES	Sweet, mild flavor like that of onion. Excellent in salads, fish, soups and potatoes.
CILANTRO	Use fresh. Excellent in salads, fish, chicken, rice, beans and Mexican dishes.
CINNAMON	Sweet, pungent flavor. Widely used in many sweet baked goods, chocolate dishes, cheesecakes, pickles, chutneys and hot drinks.
CORIANDER	Mild, sweet, orangy flavor and available whole or ground. Common in curry powders and pickling spice and also used in chutney, meat dishes, casseroles, Greek-style dishes, apple pies and baked goods.
CURRY POWDER	Spices are combined to proper proportions to give a distinct flavor to meat, poultry, fish and vegetables.
DILL	Both seeds and leaves are flavorful. Leaves may be used as a garnish or cooked with fish, soup, dressings, potatoes and beans. Leaves or the whole plant may be used to flavor pickles.
FENNEL	Sweet, hot flavor. Both seeds and leaves are used. Use in small quantities in pies and baked goods. Leaves can be boiled with fish.

HERBS & SPICES

GINGER
A pungent root, this aromatic spice is sold fresh, dried or ground. Use in pickles, preserves, cakes, cookies, soups and meat dishes.

MARJORAM
May be used both dried or green. Use to flavor fish, poultry, omelets, lamb, stew, stuffing and tomato juice.

MINT
Aromatic with a cool flavor. Excellent in beverages, fish, lamb, cheese, soup, peas, carrots and fruit desserts.

NUTMEG
Whole or ground. Used in chicken and cream soups, cheese dishes, fish cakes, and with chicken and veal. Excellent in custards, milk puddings, pies and cakes.

OREGANO
Strong, aromatic odor. Use whole or ground in tomato juice, fish, eggs, pizza, omelets, chili, stew, gravy, poultry and vegetables.

PAPRIKA
A bright red pepper, this spice is used in meat, vegetables and soups or as a garnish for potatoes, salads or eggs.

PARSLEY
Best when used fresh, but can be used dried as a garnish or as a seasoning. Try in fish, omelets, soup, meat, stuffing and mixed greens.

ROSEMARY
Very aromatic. Can be used fresh or dried. Season fish, stuffing, beef, lamb, poultry, onions, eggs, bread and potatoes. Great in dressings.

SAFFRON
Aromatic, slightly bitter taste. Only a pinch needed to flavor and color dishes such as bouillabaisse, chicken soup, rice, paella, fish sauces, buns and cakes. Very expensive, so where a touch of color is needed, use turmeric instead, but the flavor will not be the same.

SAGE
Use fresh or dried. The flowers are sometimes used in salads. May be used in tomato juice, fish, omelets, beef, poultry, stuffing, cheese spreads and breads.

TARRAGON
Leaves have a pungent, hot taste. Use to flavor sauces, salads, fish, poultry, tomatoes, eggs, green beans, carrots and dressings.

THYME
Sprinkle leaves on fish or poultry before broiling or baking. Throw a few sprigs directly on coals shortly before meat is finished grilling.

TURMERIC
Aromatic, slightly bitter flavor. Should be used sparingly in curry powder and relishes and to color cakes and rice dishes.

Use 3 times more fresh herbs if substituting fresh for dried.

BAKING BREADS

HINTS FOR BAKING BREADS

- Kneading dough for 30 seconds after mixing improves the texture of baking powder biscuits.

- Instead of shortening, use cooking or salad oil in waffles and hot cakes.

- When bread is baking, a small dish of water in the oven will help keep the crust from hardening.

- Dip a spoon in hot water to measure shortening, butter, etc., and the fat will slip out more easily.

- Small amounts of leftover corn may be added to pancake batter for variety.

- To make bread crumbs, use the fine cutter of a food grinder and tie a large paper bag over the spout in order to prevent flying crumbs.

- When you are doing any sort of baking, you get better results if you remember to preheat your cookie sheet, muffin tins or cake pans.

3 RULES FOR USE OF LEAVENING AGENTS

1. In simple flour mixtures, use 2 teaspoons baking powder to leaven 1 cup flour. Reduce this amount 1/2 teaspoon for each egg used.

2. To 1 teaspoon soda, use 2 1/4 teaspoons cream of tartar, 2 cups freshly soured milk or 1 cup molasses.

3. To substitute soda and an acid for baking powder, divide the amount of baking powder by 4. Take that as your measure and add acid according to rule 2.

PROPORTIONS OF BAKING POWDER TO FLOUR

biscuits ....to 1 cup flour use 1 1/4 tsp. baking powder
cake with oil ....to 1 cup flour use 1 tsp. baking powder
muffins ....to 1 cup flour use 1 1/2 tsp. baking powder
popovers ....to 1 cup flour use 1 1/4 tsp. baking powder
waffles ....to 1 cup flour use 1 1/4 tsp. baking powder

PROPORTIONS OF LIQUID TO FLOUR

pour batter ....to 1 cup liquid use 1 cup flour
drop batter ....to 1 cup liquid use 2 to 2 1/2 cups flour
soft dough ....to 1 cup liquid use 3 to 3 1/2 cups flour
stiff dough ....to 1 cup liquid use 4 cups flour

TIME & TEMPERATURE CHART

Breads	Minutes	Temperature
biscuits	12 - 15	400° - 450°
cornbread	25 - 30	400° - 425°
gingerbread	40 - 50	350° - 370°
loaf	50 - 60	350° - 400°
nut bread	50 - 75	350°
popovers	30 - 40	425° - 450°
rolls	20 - 30	400° - 450°

BAKING DESSERTS

PERFECT COOKIES

Cookie dough that must be rolled is much easier to handle after it has been refrigerated for 10 to 30 minutes. This keeps the dough from sticking, even though it may be soft. If not done, the soft dough may require more flour and too much flour makes cookies hard and brittle. Place on a floured board only as much dough as can be easily managed. Flour the rolling pin slightly and roll lightly to desired thickness. Cut shapes close together and add trimmings to dough that needs to be rolled. Place pans or sheets in upper third of oven. Watch cookies carefully while baking in order to avoid burned edges. When sprinkling sugar on cookies, try putting it into a salt shaker in order to save time.

PERFECT PIES

- Pie crust will be better and easier to make if all the ingredients are cool.

- The lower crust should be placed in the pan so that it covers the surface smoothly. Air pockets beneath the surface will push the crust out of shape while baking.

- Folding the top crust over the lower crust before crimping will keep juices in the pie.

- When making custard pie, bake at a high temperature for about 10 minutes to prevent a soggy crust. Then finish baking at a low temperature.

- When making cream pie, sprinkle crust with powdered sugar in order to prevent it from becoming soggy.

PERFECT CAKES

- Fill cake pans two-thirds full and spread batter into corners and sides, leaving a slight hollow in the center.

- Cake is done when it shrinks from the sides of the pan or if it springs back when touched lightly with the finger.

- After removing a cake from the oven, place it on a rack for about 5 minutes. Then, the sides should be loosened and the cake turned out on a rack in order to finish cooling.

- Do not frost cakes until thoroughly cool.

- Icing will remain where you put it if you sprinkle cake with powdered sugar first.

TIME & TEMPERATURE CHART

Dessert	Time	Temperature
butter cake, layer	20-40 min.	380° - 400°
butter cake, loaf	40-60 min.	360° - 400°
cake, angel	50-60 min.	300° - 360°
cake, fruit	3-4 hrs.	275° - 325°
cake, sponge	40-60 min.	300° - 350°
cookies, molasses	18-20 min.	350° - 375°
cookies, thin	10-12 min.	380° - 390°
cream puffs	45-60 min.	300° - 350°
meringue	40-60 min.	250° - 300°
pie crust	20-40 min.	400° - 500°

VEGETABLES & FRUITS

COOKING TIME TABLE

Vegetable	Cooking Method	Time
artichokes	boiled	40 min.
	steamed	45-60 min.
asparagus tips	boiled	10-15 min.
beans, lima	boiled	20-40 min.
	steamed	60 min.
beans, string	boiled	15-35 min.
	steamed	60 min.
beets, old	boiled or steamed	1-2 hours.
beets, young with skin	boiled	30 min.
	steamed	60 min.
	baked	70-90 min.
broccoli, flowerets	boiled	5-10 min.
broccoli, stems	boiled	20-30 min.
brussels sprouts	boiled	20-30 min.
cabbage, chopped	boiled	10-20 min.
	steamed	25 min.
carrots, cut across	boiled	8-10 min.
	steamed	40 min.
cauliflower, flowerets	boiled	8-10 min.
cauliflower, stem down	boiled	20-30 min.
corn, green, tender	boiled	5-10 min.
	steamed	15 min.
	baked	20 min.
corn on the cob	boiled	8-10 min.
	steamed	15 min.
eggplant, whole	boiled	30 min.
	steamed	40 min.
	baked	45 min.
parsnips	boiled	25-40 min.
	steamed	60 min.
	baked	60-75 min.
peas, green	boiled or steamed	5-15 min.
potatoes	boiled	20-40 min.
	steamed	60 min.
	baked	45-60 min.
pumpkin or squash	boiled	20-40 min.
	steamed	45 min.
	baked	60 min.
tomatoes	boiled	5-15 min.
turnips	boiled	25-40 min.

DRYING TIME TABLE

Fruit	Sugar or Honey	Cooking Time
apricots	¼ c. for each cup of fruit	about 40 min.
figs	1 T. for each cup of fruit	about 30 min.
peaches	¼ c. for each cup of fruit	about 45 min.
prunes	2 T. for each cup of fruit	about 45 min.

VEGETABLES & FRUITS

BUYING FRESH VEGETABLES

Artichokes: Look for compact, tightly closed heads with green, clean-looking leaves. Avoid those with leaves that are brown or separated.

Asparagus: Stalks should be tender and firm; tips should be close and compact. Choose the stalks with very little white; they are more tender. Use asparagus soon because it toughens quickly.

Beans, Snap: Those with small seeds inside the pods are best. Avoid beans with dry-looking pods.

Broccoli, Brussels Sprouts and Cauliflower: Flower clusters on broccoli and cauliflower should be tight and close together. Brussels sprouts should be firm and compact. Smudgy, dirty spots may indicate pests or disease.

Cabbage and Head Lettuce: Choose heads that are heavy for their size. Avoid cabbage with worm holes and lettuce with discoloration or soft rot.

Cucumbers: Choose long, slender cucumbers for best quality. May be dark or medium green, but yellow ones are undesirable.

Mushrooms: Caps should be closed around the stems. Avoid black or brown gills.

Peas and Lima Beans: Select pods that are well-filled but not bulging. Avoid dried, spotted, yellow or limp pods.

BUYING FRESH FRUITS

Bananas: Skin should be free of bruises and black or brown spots. Purchase them slightly green and allow them to ripen at room temperature.

Berries: Select plump, solid berries with good color. Avoid stained containers which indicate wet or leaky berries. Berries with clinging caps, such as blackberries and raspberries, may be unripe. Strawberries without caps may be overripe.

Melons: In cantaloupes, thick, close netting on the rind indicates best quality. Cantaloupes are ripe when the stem scar is smooth and the space between the netting is yellow or yellow-green. They are best when fully ripe with fruity odor.

Honeydews are ripe when rind has creamy to yellowish color and velvety texture. Immature honeydews are whitish-green.

Ripe watermelons have some yellow color on one side. If melons are white or pale green on one side, they are not ripe.

Oranges, Grapefruit and Lemons: Choose those heavy for their size. Smoother, thinner skins usually indicate more juice. Most skin markings do not affect quality. Oranges with a slight greenish tinge may be just as ripe as fully colored ones. Light or greenish-yellow lemons are more tart than deep yellow ones. Avoid citrus fruits showing withered, sunken or soft areas.

NAPKIN FOLDING

FOR BEST RESULTS, use well-starched linen napkins if possible. For more complicated folds, 24-inch napkins work best. Practice the folds with newspapers. Children will have fun decorating the table once they learn these attractive folds!

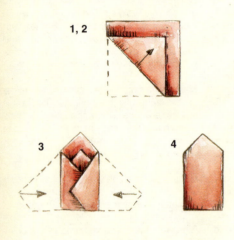

SHIELD

Easy fold. Elegant with monogram in corner.

Instructions:
1. Fold into quarter size. If monogrammed, ornate corner should face down.
2. Turn up folded corner three-quarters.
3. Overlap right side and left side points.
4. Turn over; adjust sides so they are even, single point in center.
5. Place point up or down on plate, or left of plate.

ROSETTE

Elegant on plate.

Instructions:
1. Fold left and right edges to center, leaving 1/2" opening along center.
2. Pleat firmly from top edge to bottom edge. Sharpen edges with hot iron.
3. Pinch center together. If necessary, use small piece of pipe cleaner to secure and top with single flower.
4. Spread out rosette.

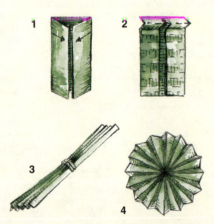

NAPKIN FOLDING

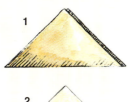

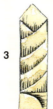

CANDLE
Easy to do; can be decorated.

Instructions:
1. Fold into triangle, point at top.
2. Turn lower edge up 1".
3. Turn over, folded edge down.
4. Roll tightly from left to right.
5. Tuck in corner. Stand upright.

FAN
Pretty in napkin ring or on plate.

Instructions:
1. Fold top and bottom edges to center.
2. Fold top and bottom edges to center a second time.
3. Pleat firmly from the left edge. Sharpen edges with hot iron.
4. Spread out fan. Balance flat folds of each side on table. Well-starched napkins will hold shape.

LILY
Effective and pretty on table.

Instructions:
1. Fold napkin into quarters.
2. Fold into triangle, closed corner to open points.
3. Turn two points over to other side. (Two points are on either side of closed point.)
4. Pleat.
5. Place closed end in glass. Pull down two points on each side and shape.

MEASUREMENTS & SUBSTITUTIONS

MEASUREMENTS

a pinch	1/8 teaspoon or less
3 teaspoons	1 tablespoon
4 tablespoons	1/4 cup
8 tablespoons	1/2 cup
12 tablespoons	3/4 cup
16 tablespoons	1 cup
2 cups	1 pint
4 cups	1 quart
4 quarts	1 gallon
8 quarts	1 peck
4 pecks	1 bushel
16 ounces	1 pound
32 ounces	1 quart
1 ounce liquid	2 tablespoons
8 ounces liquid	1 cup

Use standard measuring spoons and cups. All measurements are level.

C° TO F° CONVERSION

120° C	250° F
140° C	275° F
150° C	300° F
160° C	325° F
180° C	350° F
190° C	375° F
200° C	400° F
220° C	425° F
230° C	450° F

Temperature conversions are estimates.

SUBSTITUTIONS

Ingredient	Quantity	Substitute
baking powder	1 teaspoon	1/4 tsp. baking soda plus 1/2 tsp. cream of tartar
chocolate	1 square (1 oz.)	3 or 4 T. cocoa plus 1 T. butter
cornstarch	1 tablespoon	2 T. flour or 2 tsp. quick-cooking tapioca
cracker crumbs	3/4 cup	1 c. bread crumbs
dates	1 lb.	1 1/2 c. dates, pitted and cut
dry mustard	1 teaspoon	1 T. prepared mustard
flour, self-rising	1 cup	1 c. all-purpose flour, 1/2 tsp. salt, and 1 tsp. baking powder
herbs, fresh	1 tablespoon	1 tsp. dried herbs
ketchup or chili sauce	1 cup	1 c. tomato sauce plus 1/2 c. sugar and 2 T. vinegar (for use in cooking)
milk, sour	1 cup	1 T. lemon juice or vinegar plus sweet milk to make 1 c. (let stand 5 minutes)
whole	1 cup	1/2 c. evaporated milk plus 1/2 c. water
min. marshmallows	10	1 lg. marshmallow
onion, fresh	1 small	1 T. instant minced onion, rehydrated
sugar, brown	1/2 cup	2 T. molasses in 1/2 c. granulated sugar
powdered	1 cup	1 c. granulated sugar plus 1 tsp. cornstarch
tomato juice	1 cup	1/2 c. tomato sauce plus 1/2 c. water

When substituting cocoa for chocolate in cakes, the amount of flour must be reduced. Brown and white sugars usually can be interchanged.

SUGAR

EQUIVALENCY CHART

Food	Quantity	Yield
apple	1 medium	1 cup
banana, mashed	1 medium	1/3 cup
bread	1 1/2 slices	1 cup soft crumbs
bread	1 slice	1/4 cup fine, dry crumbs
butter	1 stick or 1/4 pound	1/2 cup
cheese, American, cubed	1 pound	2 2/3 cups
American, grated	1 pound	5 cups
cream cheese	3-ounce package	6 2/3 tablespoons
chocolate, bitter	1 square	1 ounce
cocoa	1 pound	4 cups
coconut	1 1/2 pound package	2 2/3 cups
coffee, ground	1 pound	5 cups
cornmeal	1 pound	3 cups
cornstarch	1 pound	3 cups
crackers, graham	14 squares	1 cup fine crumbs
saltine	28 crackers	1 cup fine crumbs
egg	4-5 whole	1 cup
whites	8-10	1 cup
yolks	10-12	1 cup
evaporated milk	1 cup	3 cups whipped
flour, cake, sifted	1 pound	4 1/2 cups
rye	1 pound	5 cups
white, sifted	1 pound	4 cups
white, unsifted	1 pound	3 3/4 cups
gelatin, flavored	3 1/4 ounces	1/2 cup
unflavored	1/4 ounce	1 tablespoon
lemon	1 medium	3 tablespoon juice
marshmallows	16	1/4 pound
noodles, cooked	8-ounce package	7 cups
uncooked	4 ounces (1 1/2 cups)	2-3 cups cooked
macaroni, cooked	8-ounce package	6 cups
macaroni, uncooked	4 ounces (1 1/4 cups)	2 1/4 cups cooked
spaghetti, uncooked	7 ounces	4 cups cooked
nuts, chopped	1/4 pound	1 cup
almonds	1 pound	3 1/2 cups
walnuts, broken	1 pound	3 cups
walnuts, unshelled	1 pound	1 1/2 to 1 3/4 cups
onion	1 medium	1/2 cup
orange	3-4 medium	1 cup juice
raisins	1 pound	3 1/2 cups
rice, brown	1 cup	4 cups cooked
converted	1 cup	3 1/2 cups cooked
regular	1 cup	3 cups cooked
wild	1 cup	4 cups cooked
sugar, brown	1 pound	2 1/2 cups
powdered	1 pound	3 1/2 cups
white	1 pound	2 cups
vanilla wafers	22	1 cup fine crumbs
zwieback, crumbled	4	1 cups

FOOD QUANTITIES

FOR LARGE SERVINGS

	25 Servings	50 Servings	100 Servings

Beverages:
- coffee .... 1/2 pound and 1 1/2 gallons water .... 1 pound and 3 gallons water .... 2 pounds and 6 gallons water
- lemonade .... 10-15 lemons and 1 1/2 gallons water .... 20-30 lemons and 3 gallons water .... 40-60 lemons and 6 gallons water
- tea .... 1/12 pound and 1 1/2 gallons water .... 1/6 pound and 3 gallons water .... 1/3 pound and 6 gallons water

Desserts:
- layered cake .... 1 12" cake .... 3 10" cakes .... 6 10" cakes
- sheet cake .... 1 10" x 12" cake .... 1 12" x 20" cake .... 2 12" x 20" cakes
- watermelon .... 37 1/2 pounds .... 75 pounds .... 150 pounds
- whipping cream .... 3/4 pint .... 1 1/2 to 2 pints .... 3-4 pints

Ice cream:
- brick .... 3 1/4 quarts .... 6 1/2 quarts .... 13 quarts
- bulk .... 2 1/4 quarts .... 4 1/2 quarts or 1 1/4 gallons .... 9 quarts or 2 1/2 gallons

Meat, poultry or fish:
- fish .... 13 pounds .... 25 pounds .... 50 pounds
- fish, fillets or steak ...... 7 1/2 pounds ...... 15 pounds ...... 30 pounds
- hamburger .... 9 pounds .... 18 pounds .... 35 pounds
- turkey or chicken .... 13 pounds .... 25 to 35 pounds .... 50 to 75 pounds
- wieners (beef) .... 6 1/2 pounds .... 13 pounds .... 25 pounds

Salads, casseroles:
- baked beans .... 3/4 gallon .... 1 1/4 gallons .... 2 1/2 gallons
- jello salad .... 3/4 gallon .... 1 1/4 gallons .... 2 1/2 gallons
- potato salad .... 4 1/4 quarts .... 2 1/4 gallons .... 4 1/2 gallons
- scalloped potatoes .... 4 1/2 quarts or 1 12" x 20" pan .... 9 quarts or 2 1/4 gallons .... 18 quarts 4 1/2 gallons
- spaghetti .... 1 1/4 gallons .... 2 1/2 gallons .... 5 gallons

Sandwiches:
- bread .... 50 slices or 3 1-pound loaves .... 100 slices or 6 1-pound loaves .... 200 slices or 12 1-pound loaves
- butter .... 1/2 pound .... 1 pound .... 2 pounds
- lettuce .... 1 1/2 heads .... 3 heads .... 6 heads
- mayonnaise .... 1 cup .... 2 cups .... 4 cups
- mixed filling
  - meat, eggs, fish ...... 1 1/2 quarts ...... 3 quarts ...... 6 quarts
  - jam, jelly .... 1 quart .... 2 quarts .... 4 quarts

QUICK FIXES

PRACTICALLY EVERYONE has experienced that dreadful moment in the kitchen when a recipe failed and dinner guests have arrived. Perhaps a failed timer, distraction or a missing or mismeasured ingredient is to blame. These handy tips can save the day!

Acidic foods – Sometimes a tomato-based sauce will become too acidic. Add baking soda, one teaspoon at a time, to the sauce. Use sugar as a sweeter alternative.

Burnt food on pots and pans – Allow the pan to cool on its own. Remove as much of the food as possible. Fill with hot water and add a capful of liquid fabric softener to the pot; let it stand for a few hours. You'll have an easier time removing the burnt food.

Chocolate seizes – Chocolate can seize (turn coarse and grainy) when it comes into contact with water. Place seized chocolate in a metal bowl over a large saucepan with an inch of simmering water in it. Over medium heat, slowly whisk in warm heavy cream. Use 1/4 cup cream to 4 ounces of chocolate. The chocolate will melt and become smooth.

Forgot to thaw whipped topping – Thaw in microwave for 1 minute on the defrost setting. Stir to blend well. Do not over thaw!

Hands smell like garlic or onion – Rinse hands under cold water while rubbing them with a large stainless steel spoon.

Hard brown sugar – Place in a paper bag and microwave for a few seconds, or place hard chunks in a food processor.

Jello too hard – Heat on a low microwave power setting for a very short time.

Lumpy gravy or sauce – Use a blender, food processor or simply strain.

No tomato juice – Mix 1/2 cup ketchup with 1/2 cup water.

Out of honey – Substitute 1 1/4 cups sugar dissolved in 1 cup water.

Overcooked sweet potatoes or carrots – Softened sweet potatoes and carrots make a wonderful soufflé with the addition of eggs and sugar. Consult your favorite cookbook for a good soufflé recipe. Overcooked sweet potatoes can also be used as pie filling.

Sandwich bread is stale – Toast or microwave bread briefly. Otherwise, turn it into breadcrumbs. Bread exposed to light and heat will hasten its demise, so consider using a bread box.

Soup, sauce, gravy too thin – Add 1 tablespoon of flour to hot soup, sauce or gravy. Whisk well (to avoid lumps) while the mixture is boiling. Repeat if necessary.

Sticky rice – Rinse rice with warm water.

Stew or soup is greasy – Refrigerate and remove grease once it congeals. Another trick is to lay cold lettuce leaves over the hot stew for about 10 seconds and then remove. Repeat as necessary.

Too salty – Add a little sugar and vinegar. For soups or sauces, add a raw peeled potato.

Too sweet – Add a little vinegar or lemon juice.

Undercooked cakes and cookies – Serve over vanilla ice cream. You can also layer pieces of cake or cookies with whipped cream and fresh fruit to form a dessert parfait. Crumbled cookies also make an excellent ice cream or cream pie topping.

COUNTING CALORIES

BEVERAGES

apple juice, 6 oz. 90
coffee (black) 0
cola, 12 oz. 115
cranberry juice, 6 oz. 115
ginger ale, 12 oz. 115
grape juice, (prepared from
    frozen concentrate), 6 oz. 142
lemonade, (prepared from
    frozen concentrate), 6 oz. 85
milk, protein fortified, 1 c. 105
    skim, 1 c. 90
    whole, 1 c. 160
orange juice, 6 oz. 85
pineapple juice, unsweetened, 6 oz. 95
root beer, 12 oz. 150
tonic (quinine water) 12 oz. 132

BREADS

cornbread, 1 sm. square 130
dumplings, 1 med. 70
French toast, 1 slice........................135
melba toast, 1 slice 25
muffins, blueberry, 1 muffin 110
    bran, 1 muffin..............................106
    corn, 1 muffin 125
    English, 1 muffin 280
pancakes, 1 (4-in.) 60
pumpernickel, 1 slice 75
rye, 1 slice 60
waffle, 1 216
white, 1 slice 60-70
whole wheat, 1 slice 55-65

CEREALS

cornflakes, 1 c. 105
cream of wheat, 1 c. 120
oatmeal, 1 c. 148
rice flakes, 1 c. 105
shredded wheat, 1 biscuit 100
sugar krisps, 3/4 c. 110

CRACKERS

graham, 1 cracker 15-30
rye crisp, 1 cracker...........................35
saltine, 1 cracker...........................17-20
wheat thins, 1 cracker 9

DAIRY PRODUCTS

butter or margarine, 1 T. 100
cheese, American, 1 oz. 100
    camembert, 1 oz. 85
    cheddar, 1 oz. 115
    cottage cheese, 1 oz. 30
    mozzarella, 1 oz. 90
    parmesan, 1 oz. 130
    ricotta, 1 oz. 50
    roquefort, 1 oz. 105
    Swiss, 1 oz. 105
cream, light, 1 T. 30
    heavy, 1 T. 55
    sour, 1 T. 45
hot chocolate, with milk, 1 c. 277
milk chocolate, 1 oz. 145-155
yogurt
    made w/ whole milk, 1 c. 150-165
    made w/ skimmed milk, 1 c. 125

EGGS

fried, 1 lg. 100
poached or boiled, 1 lg. 75-80
scrambled or in omelet, 1 lg. 110-130

FISH AND SEAFOOD

bass, 4 oz. 105
salmon, broiled or baked, 3 oz. 155
sardines, canned in oil, 3 oz. 170
trout, fried, 3 1/2 oz. 220
tuna, in oil, 3 oz. 170
    in water, 3 oz. 110

COUNTING CALORIES

FRUITS

apple, 1 med. 80-100
applesauce, sweetened, ½ c. 90-115
    unsweetened, ½ c. 50
banana, 1 med. 85
blueberries, ½ c. 45
cantaloupe, ½ c. 24
cherries (pitted), raw, ½ c. 40
grapefruit, ½ med. 55
grapes, ½ c. 35-55
honeydew, ½ c. 55
mango, 1 med. 90
orange, 1 med. 65-75
peach, 1 med. 35
pear, 1 med. 60-100
pineapple, fresh, ½ c. 40
    canned in syrup, ½ c. 95
plum, 1 med. 30
strawberries, fresh, ½ c. 30
    frozen and sweetened, ½ c. ..120-140
tangerine, 1 lg. 39
watermelon, ½ c. 42

MEAT AND POULTRY

beef, ground (lean), 3 oz. 185
    roast, 3 oz. 185
chicken, broiled, 3 oz. 115
lamb chop (lean), 3 oz. 175-200
steak, sirloin, 3 oz. 175
    tenderloin, 3 oz. 174
    top round, 3 oz. 162
turkey, dark meat, 3 oz. 175
    white meat, 3 oz. 150
veal, cutlet, 3 oz. 156
    roast, 3 oz. 76

NUTS

almonds, 2 T. 105
cashews, 2 T. 100
peanuts, 2 T. 105
peanut butter, 1 T. 95
pecans, 2 T. 95
pistachios, 2 T. 92
walnuts, 2 T. 80

PASTA

macaroni or spaghetti,
    cooked, ¾ c. 115

SALAD DRESSINGS

blue cheese, 1 T. 70
French, 1 T. 65
Italian, 1 T. 80
mayonnaise, 1 T. 100
olive oil, 1 T. 124
Russian, 1 T. 70
salad oil, 1 T. 120

SOUPS

bean, 1 c. 130-180
beef noodle, 1 c. 70
bouillon and consomme, 1 c. 30
chicken noodle, 1 c. 65
chicken with rice, 1 c. 50
minestrone, 1 c. 80-150
split pea, 1 c. 145-170
tomato with milk, 1 c. 170
vegetable, 1 c. 80-100

VEGETABLES

asparagus, 1 c. 35
broccoli, cooked, ½ c. 25
cabbage, cooked, ½ c. 15-20
carrots, cooked, ½ c. 25-30
cauliflower, ½ c. 10-15
corn (kernels), ½ c. 70
green beans, 1 c. 30
lettuce, shredded, ½ c. 5
mushrooms, canned, ½ c. 20
onions, cooked, ½ c. 30
peas, cooked, ½ c. 60
potato, baked, 1 med. 90
    chips, 8-10 100
    mashed, w/milk & butter, 1 c. ..200-300
spinach, 1 c. 40
tomato, raw, 1 med. 25
    cooked, ½ c. 30

COOKING TERMS

Au gratin: Topped with crumbs and/or cheese and browned in oven or under broiler.

Au jus: Served in its own juices.

Baste: To moisten foods during cooking with pan drippings or special sauce in order to add flavor and prevent drying.

Bisque: A thick cream soup.

Blanch: To immerse in rapidly boiling water and allow to cook slightly.

Cream: To soften a fat, especially butter, by beating it at room temperature. Butter and sugar are often creamed together, making a smooth, soft paste.

Crimp: To seal the edges of a two-crust pie either by pinching them at intervals with the fingers or by pressing them together with the tines of a fork.

Crudites: An assortment of raw vegetables (i.e. carrots, broccoli, celery, mushrooms) that is served as an hors d'oeuvre, often accompanied by a dip.

Degrease: To remove fat from the surface of stews, soups or stock. Usually cooled in the refrigerator so that fat hardens and is easily removed.

Dredge: To coat lightly with flour, cornmeal, etc.

Entree: The main course.

Fold: To incorporate a delicate substance, such as whipped cream or beaten egg whites, into another substance without releasing air bubbles. A spatula is used to gently bring part of the mixture from the bottom of the bowl to the top. The process is repeated, while slowly rotating the bowl, until the ingredients are thoroughly blended.

Glaze: To cover with a glossy coating, such as a melted and somewhat diluted jelly for fruit desserts.

Julienne: To cut or slice vegetables, fruits or cheeses into match-shaped slivers.

Marinate: To allow food to stand in a liquid in order to tenderize or to add flavor.

Meuniére: Dredged with flour and sautéed in butter.

Mince: To chop food into very small pieces.

Parboil: To boil until partially cooked; to blanch. Usually final cooking in a seasoned sauce follows this procedure.

Pare: To remove the outermost skin of a fruit or vegetable.

Poach: To cook gently in hot liquid kept just below the boiling point.

Purée: To mash foods by hand by rubbing through a sieve or food mill, or by whirling in a blender or food processor until perfectly smooth.

Refresh: To run cold water over food that has been parboiled in order to stop the cooking process quickly.

Sauté: To cook and/or brown food in a small quantity of hot shortening.

Scald: To heat to just below the boiling point, when tiny bubbles appear at the edge of the saucepan.

Simmer: To cook in liquid just below the boiling point. The surface of the liquid should be barely moving, broken from time to time by slowly rising bubbles.

Steep: To let food stand in hot liquid in order to extract or to enhance flavor, like tea in hot water or poached fruit in syrup.

Toss: To combine ingredients with a repeated lifting motion.

Whip: To beat rapidly in order to incorporate air and produce expansion, as in heavy cream or egg whites.

Publish your own Cookbook

Churches, schools, organizations, and families can preserve their favorite recipes by publishing a custom cookbook. Cookbooks make a great **fundraiser** because they are easy to sell and highly profitable. Our low prices also make cookbooks a perfect affordable **keepsake**. We offer:

- Low prices, high quality, and prompt service.
- Many options and styles to suit your needs.
- 90 days to pay and a written No-Risk Guarantee.

Order our FREE Cookbook Kit for full details:

- Call us at **800-445-6621, ext. CB**.
- Visit our web site at **www.morriscookbooks.com**.
- Mail the **postage-paid reply card** below.

Discover the right ingredients for a really great cookbook!

Order our **FREE** Cookbook Kit. Please print neatly.

Name _____

Organization _____

Address _____

City _____ State _____ Zip _____

E-mail _____

Phone (_____) _____

P. O. Box 2110
Kearney, NE 68848

Back Card 8-09

You supply the recipes and we'll do the rest!™

Whether your goal is to raise funds or simply create a cherished keepsake, Morris Press Cookbooks has all the right ingredients to make a great custom cookbook. Raise $500–$50,000 while preserving favorite recipes.

Three ways to order our **FREE** Cookbook Kit:
- Call us at **800-445-6621, ext. CB**.
- Visit our web site at **www.morriscookbooks.com**.
- Complete and mail the **postage-paid reply card** below.

BUSINESS REPLY MAIL
FIRST-CLASS MAIL   PERMIT NO. 36   KEARNEY, NE

POSTAGE WILL BE PAID BY ADDRESSEE

Morris Press Cookbooks
P.O. Box 2110
Kearney, NE 68848-9985